I Hate It When
EXERCISE
Is the Answer

Other Titles by Emily Watts

I Hate It When
EXERCISE
Is the Answer

A Fitness Program for the Soul

— • • • • • • • • • —

Emily Watts

ᴹᴹ ®

DESERET
BOOK

Library of Congress Cataloging-in-Publication Data

Watts, Emily.
    I hate it when exercise is the answer : a fitness program for the soul
/ Emily Watts.
        p. cm.
    Includes bibliographical references.
    ISBN 978-1-60641-107-0 (paperbound)
    1. Christian life—Mormon authors.   I. Title.
    BX8656.W38 2009
    248.8'43—dc22   2009005707

Printed in the United States of America
Edward Brothers Incorporated, Lillington, NC

10   9   8   7   6   5   4   3   2

To Rachel, Benjamin, Tyler,
and all the grandchildren yet to come.
I'm exercising to keep up with you.

CONTENTS

Contents

Contents

INTRODUCTION

When Exercise Is the Answer

When I turned fifty, some of my more smart-alecky friends were quick to inform me that the warranty on my body had now expired, and I could expect things to start breaking down on a regular basis. I laughed it off at first, but it wasn't long before their predictions began to be realized.

It started with the day I finally succumbed to the inevitability of bifocals. I'd hardly even noticed that my glasses were no longer helping with close-range vision until one day when my family was playing a game where you have to read something quickly off a little card and I yanked my glasses off in exasperation in order to see the words.

It was downhill from there. I noticed that I got tired more

1

easily. It was harder to get out of bed in the morning, and my ankles were often swollen at the end of the day. I could no longer devour with impunity half a dozen chocolate-chip cookies or even one entire Cinnabon. Such indulgences, which had previously been a given in my life, would now set me up for the most miserable few hours afterward. (You'd think that letting go of them would have made some difference to my weight, but no such luck.)

The worst problem was a series of kidney infections that would flare up when I was particularly stressed about something. The first, which struck without warning, landed me in the emergency room and ultimately required repeated intravenous infusions of antibiotics to bring it under control. After about six bouts, one every few months, the doctor called me in and said, "I've been looking over your lab reports, and I don't think your problem has been with your kidneys in more than two of these incidents. I think what you're experiencing is actually lower back pain, and I'd like to send you to a physical therapist who can teach you some exercises to prevent it."

Exercise. Why did exercise have to be the answer?

I *hate* it when exercise is the answer—and, particularly when you're over fifty, it seems like it's always the answer. Pick up any women's magazine and leaf through it. Wanting to shed a few pounds or lose two dress sizes before the holidays or get in shape for swimsuit season? Exercise. Trying to prevent Type 2 diabetes? Exercise. Hoping to ward off a heart attack? Exercise. Working to shake off depression? Exercise. And my favorite: Feeling fatigued? Exercise. Yeah, right. How am I supposed to exercise when I'm feeling so fatigued? Why is *chocolate* never the answer for any of these ailments?

I had to laugh when my married daughter called to tell me that she and her husband had gone for full physicals for the first time since their marriage. His BMI, or body mass index, the latest word in height-to-weight ratios, was a little high, but the doctor told him it would be simple for him to drop a few pounds if he would—you guessed it—exercise.

Then it was her turn. Her BMI was actually a bit low, and the doctor told her she would be healthier and feel better if she could increase it a little. The best way for her to accomplish this, he said, would be for her to build up her lean muscle mass. How to do so? Exercise.

It's like a bad dream, isn't it?

Anyway, returning to my problem with my back, I went to the physical therapist on the appointed day. His name was Steve, and I estimated his age at about twelve. Well, not really, but health-care professionals are starting to seem awfully young to me. That used to bother me, but now I prefer it; I don't want to be breaking in any new doctors anymore. I want to have a physician who will outlive me—and Dr. Steve certainly qualified.

He started by having me walk back and forth across the room, which was surprisingly unnerving, as I was self-conscious about what he might be observing in my gait. Then he had me try a few simple exercises while he made notes that I'm sure read something like "Pitiful. This woman is barely able to move. Does she *ever* walk *anywhere?*" The worst one was when he instructed me to lie flat on my back and place my hands on my abdominal muscles, and I couldn't find them.

"I don't think I have any abdominal muscles left," I ventured sheepishly.

"Oh, you have them all right," he grinned. "You just haven't met them in a while."

When we were all finished with this torture, Dr. Steve set down his notebook, sighed, and said, "Well, you're not twenty anymore." *Brilliant diagnosis, doctor. Thank you so much for pointing that out.* Of course, he didn't mean to be unkind. It was just that, as with an older car, I needed to be more mindful to take care of my body. I couldn't expect it to function as it had when I was younger.

However, there was plenty of opportunity for improvement.

This is what Dr. Steve told me: "I'm going to give you some exercises that you might think have nothing to do with your back. There are groups of muscles in your body that we call 'core muscles,' and they steady your frame and keep everything lined up properly. When the core muscles are weak, other muscles have to compensate and take over functions they weren't designed to perform, so they can't work at their peak efficiency and they get stretched in unnatural ways. That's why you're feeling pain. The exercises I'm going to prescribe for you are designed to strengthen the core. Once we get that right, your other muscles should feel much better."

Strengthen the core. The phrase was an epiphany for me. It struck me as such a powerful image not just for physical issues but for all of life. When the core is strong, everything works as it should. When it's weak, life is harder than it needs to be.

With that concept in mind, I've developed a "fitness program for the soul," designed to strengthen my emotional and spiritual core. Just as I have to do my physical therapy exercises to keep my core muscles from breaking down, I find that I need regular reminders to keep myself emotionally and spiritually fit. I've come up with thirty-one simple exercises that help me accomplish this, one for each day of even the longest month. I'm hoping there might be something here that will help you too.

As much as I hate to admit it, it turns out that exercise really is the answer for a whole host of ills. That being the case, we might as well have fun along the way!

1

What Was the First Straw?

An Exercise in Releasing Pressure

We were undergoing this "wellness challenge" at work, and the goal for the month was to drink some ridiculous amount of water every day. I can't remember how much it was; I remember only that I felt completely waterlogged and bloated when I tried to do it. So when I was in the store and noticed "flavored sparkling water" on the shelf, I picked up a bunch of bottles to help me reach my water-drinking goal.

Upon reflection and experience, I've decided that *flavored sparkling water* is code for *diet soda*. It appears to have sweeteners and flavoring ingredients identical to those in diet soda. And, although "sparkling water" somehow *sounds* healthier, I'm pretty sure it isn't. At least it doesn't have any artificial coloring. That's got to count for something, right? Regrettably, I'm quite sure it doesn't count in the water assessment for the wellness challenge.

I like it, though. It has just one drawback, which I discovered the first time I tried it: When that label says *sparkling*, it's not kidding. This stuff explodes when you open the bottle like no soft drink I've ever experienced. (It's surprisingly non-sticky, which is fortunate. I guess aspartame doesn't have the same tacky properties as sugar.)

I soon learned that the best strategy when opening a new bottle of sparkling water is to screw off the lid just a little, let some of the bubbles out, and then screw it back on really quickly before they all come rushing to the top. Several repetitions of that action are generally enough to calm the drink down so it can be opened all the way without incident.

It struck me one day as I was taming a bottle of sparkling water that my life is like that sometimes. There are days when the pressure has built up so tremendously that the slightest thing will trigger a rather messy explosion. Maybe if I could find some ways to "let some of the bubbles out," I could avoid embarrassing myself and upsetting my family.

I remember one such time when I was apologizing to my children after having blown up at them over some minor infraction. Recognizing from the perplexed look on their faces that they really didn't know what had hit them (or why), I said to my daughter, "Oh, honey, it wasn't really what you guys did. It was just the last straw, that's all."

She looked at me thoughtfully for a moment and then asked, "Mom, what was the first straw?"

Hmm. Pretty insightful question, I thought, and one that I would do well to ask myself when things seem to be raging out of control. What is piling up here? What do I need to unload so that I can function normally? More to the point— how do I do it?

The most important thing I've discovered is that I can't deal with the whole pile of straw or the whole bottleful of bubbles all at once. It's just too much. It explodes. I have to do something to let a little pressure out, then a little more, and so on until it's safe to proceed.

Sometimes I just close the door to my office or bedroom and give myself a few seconds for a silent scream. Have you tried this? I know it seems gimmicky, but you might be amazed at how cathartic it can be. Clench your fists, tighten your stomach, open your mouth wide, and just let loose— but don't let any noise come out. In fact, if you don't bother to retreat to another room and just do this in full sight of the children, it will likely make them laugh, and then whatever they were fighting about might just dissolve on its own.

(I don't recommend that degree of openness at work, though. In public, the technique is better relegated to a closed office or, if all else fails, a bathroom stall.)

Another thing I like to do when I'm under a lot of pressure is take time to make a list. This helps me see the individual stressors for what they are, and I'm much more able to make a rational decision about how to deal with them. A lot of them just slink away right off the list when they see how silly they look in black and white. Others line themselves up in a more orderly fashion instead of bouncing around demanding to be coped with all at once.

Spending five minutes outside, particularly if there's sunshine out there, can make a world of difference. There's just something about a change in air quality that shakes things loose and releases a few of those bubbles.

Having something pleasant planned at the end of a long day makes getting through the daily grind more bearable. Sometimes I write myself an encouraging little sticky note: "Play tickets tonight" or "Brownies for dessert" or "Grandbabies coming Saturday!" It serves as a nice reminder that life isn't always as bleak as it seems at the moment, which is hard to remember when you're mired in the bleakness.

My favorite pressure-releasing strategy is just to laugh. Watch a funny YouTube clip. Keep a folder of those silly e-mails people are always circulating, and pull one out for another chuckle. Call a friend and say, "Remember when . . . ?" Let it out, and you'll go forward renewed and refreshed and a lot better equipped to handle whatever life throws at you.

Exercise #1: Releasing Pressure

Take a minute at the beginning of the day to assess what bubbles might be building up in the bottle that is your life. If it looks like the pressure might be high, choose one of the strategies from this chapter (or a different one that works for you) and let off some of those bubbles right now before the whole thing blows up in someone's face.

2

The Wrong Bus

An Exercise in Forgiving

Last year my husband, Larry, and I got to go on an Alaskan cruise, a wonderful and unforgettable experience that we will always treasure. It was the last cruising weekend of the season, we were told, so every cruise line had its farewell voyage going, and in every port the ships from the various companies were lined up along the dock.

In Skagway, it looked as if our ship was probably anchored close enough for us to walk to town, but as we started along, a little shuttle bus came by and offered us a lift for $1, so to conserve time and energy we hopped aboard. We spent some time in a marvelous little museum, stepped into a few shops, and wandered around for a while, watching the clock because we were booked to take the White Mountain Scenic Railway tour up the mountainside at 12:40 and had to be back to the dock twenty minutes before the tour left. I figured we ought to catch a bus back around noon, so at that hour we walked out to the nearest stop, and soon a shuttle came along.

As others were climbing aboard, I heard the bus driver say, "If you're not going to the *VeenDam,* this is not your bus." We were on the *Celebrity Millennium.* So I backed out of the queue and told Larry we weren't supposed to get on that bus. It pulled away, not even half full, and we were frustrated because, after all, the shuttles would all end up at the pier anyway, wouldn't they? What difference did it make if the bus didn't go all the way down to our ship? We could surely walk the few extra steps. Why did they have these stupid rules? We decided that they must be trying to keep the shuttle ridership evened out, but since there didn't seem to be any space issues at this particular hour, we should have just gotten on that bus.

Well, soon another bus pulled up with a display card in the window that again read *"VeenDam,"* but the driver was the same one who had driven us into town. He gave the same speech about this being the wrong bus if we weren't going to that particular ship, but this time we were not going to be duped. We were climbing aboard when a second bus pulled up behind us that was displaying *Celebrity Millennium* in the window. I wanted to get off our bus and switch to that one, but Larry said it was silly, so we stayed on the *VeenDam* bus. Sure enough, as we headed out of town, the bus took a right turn instead of the left turn that it seemed would have taken us toward the pier. We started to feel a little nervous, but maybe this was just a more circuitous route.

No such luck. Our hearts sank as we realized that we were being carried farther and farther away from our ship. Finally the bus stopped and let us out, and we assessed the situation. It turned out that the pier in Skagway was not built in one long, continuous line, as it had been in other ports. There were actually several different "spurs" of boardwalk, and the pier where the *VeenDam* was docked was in a wholly separate area from the *Millennium.* Looking around, we could see that we were easily half a mile away from our own destination (farther, in fact, than if we had just walked back from town and not even *taken* the bus).

With time running out, I started rushing down the pathway to get back to our own stop. Fueled by my anger and frustration, I was really stomping. Oh, was I *mad!* And frantic, too, that we were going to miss our train because my husband was too stubborn to listen to instructions and *I* had wanted to change busses, but *noooo,* and now we were in this mess and blah, blah, blah . . . you know how it is when you're mad at someone. A fellow who saw us hurrying along this road said to Larry, "Caught the wrong bus, huh?" and he answered, "Yes, and it was all my fault."

"You're darn right it was!" I yelled back. Stomp, stomp, stomp.

Fortunately, we got back just in time to get on the train, and after we had settled into our seats and were on our way up this gorgeous pass on the one sunny day we had in Alaska, and I was feeling the endorphins of all that fast walking, I was finally able to let go of my anger and just enjoy the time.

This is a lesson I seem destined to have to relearn over and over. I tend to hold on to things that make me mad. It seems like if I forgive my husband or my kids or my coworkers too soon, they're "getting away with something." I have to stay mad long enough to teach them a lesson, or so I tell myself. In my saner moments, I can see the fallacy in that. They're not really learning anything; they've moved on and half the time don't even realize I'm mad at them. I'm the only one being hurt by all those bad feelings I'm toting (not to mention the wear and tear on my psyche of all that emotional stomping around).

But I suspect the real reason I hold on to my anger is

because I'm afraid that if I let it go too easily, it will signal that the anger wasn't really justified in the first place. And I hate to believe that I might get angry without "just cause." I'm just starting to figure out that, although I can't always avoid feeling mad when something frustrating happens, I can certainly control what I do with that anger.

For example, I can examine where those feelings came from. Am I mad because my pride was hurt? My plans had to shift? My expectations weren't met? Maybe it's just because I'm tired, or hungry, or running behind schedule. Maybe hormones are involved. (I hate to admit how often *that* one is true!) Somehow, bringing a rational perspective to the situation often calms those fractured feelings.

Then, too, I find it useful to remind myself frequently that my husband doesn't deliberately set out to make me mad. (At least, I don't *think* he does.) In the case of the wrong bus, it was simply a matter of not understanding the reason for the rule. Either one of us could easily have clarified the situation with a simple question to the bus driver. We had assumed that the ships were lined up in a straight line, since that had been our experience in previous ports, but that had happened not to be the case in Skagway. Larry's determination to stay on that bus was not a deliberate attempt to thwart our plans; it was just a mistake. Human beings make mistakes sometimes. We have to sort through them and forgive each other when that happens.

I remember one fight my husband and I had years ago in which he yelled, "You know we're going to stay married, so we might as well work this out now!" That was just unexpected enough to make me laugh, but it was oh so true. Since we were clearly going to end up forgiving each other at some point, it made the most sense to just do it right then.

When I insist on clinging to my "righteous indignation," I'm only poisoning future experiences, holding them hostage to mistakes of the past. Much better to forgive and get on with things!

Exercise #2: Forgiving

Next time someone or something hits one of your hot buttons, let the anger wash over you for about ten seconds. Then step back, try to analyze why the experience made you mad, and make a conscious decision to forgive the person and get on with your life.

3

Instant Choirs

An Exercise in Valuing Moms

We have quite a transient ward, with lots of apartment units and young families, and it's difficult to put together a ward choir under the circumstances, although there is plenty of talent to work with. By the time the choir gets a number worked up, half the participants have moved out or are visiting their parents on the weekend of the performance or are home with sick babies or are home *having* babies . . . the list is long but the bottom line is that we don't have ward choir numbers too often.

However, our enterprising ward music director hit upon the idea once of inviting all the men in the congregation up to the choir seats to sing the intermediate hymn as an impromptu men's choir. It was actually pretty stirring. We women don't get to hear "Ye Elders of Israel" sung all that much, but the men sing it in priesthood meeting enough that they're familiar with it, and a lot of them can sing the parts, so it comes across pretty well even without advance practice.

It was such a hit, in fact, that a couple of months later our leaders decided to try it again, but with the women this time. The bishop stepped to the podium and invited all the Relief Society sisters to come to the front to perform a number for the ward. As they did so, a wail started up in the audience. Soon the only chorus that could be heard at all in the chapel was a refrain of sobs, whines, and downright screams. We sang "As Sisters in Zion," but the infants in our ward, oblivious to the music's soothing possibilities, offered a new interpretation for the phrase "we'll all work together" in their synchronized shrieking.

Think moms don't matter? Think again.

Being indispensable is part of the job of being a mom. It's exhausting and exasperating, but it can also be exhilarating. It's a great blessing to be needed. It's a wonderful gift—and a sobering responsibility—to be someone's favorite person in the world.

I remember a time when I was zoning out on my bed with the TV droning in the background, physically and emotionally spent yet again, thinking, "Why does this have to be so *hard?*" The movie playing on the television was *A League of Their Own,* in which Tom Hanks portrays the coach of a professional women's baseball team during World War II. Geena Davis, his star player, quits the team, saying, "It just got too hard."

"It's supposed to be hard," responds Hanks. "If it wasn't hard, everyone would do it. The hard is what makes it great."

What if the hard is what makes being a mom great? What if the hard is what makes *us* great? What if it's the hard that makes us grow and sends us in search of resources we didn't know we had and drives us to the arms of our Savior for answers we wouldn't have been smart enough to see ourselves?

And yet many of the best moms I know don't get how important it is, this mothering they're doing. My sweet mother-in-law was at the top of this list. She had ten children, the ninth of whom suffers from Down's syndrome. Her husband died at age 50, and she picked up alone the burden of caring for that precious daughter and the others still at home, spending almost as much of her life as a widow as she had as a bride. And still she persisted all her life in bemoaning the fact that she had never really accomplished anything.

I tried to tell her that having ten children would have been a one-way ticket to the Crazy Farm for me. Not everyone does this, I pointed out. I tried to show her how much the world had been blessed by the children she had been willing to bear and care for and love. I tried to explain that she had spent her mortality in pursuits that would matter for eternity. What were worldly "accomplishments" worth compared to that?

I don't think she ever believed me. She passed away last year, and one of my great hopes and fervent beliefs is that her perspective has now changed on this issue. Put her on one side of the room and Donald Trump on the other and let's see whose eternal empire shines the brightest.

Another of my deepest hopes is that most of us moms won't wait until we get to the other side of the veil to start recognizing what it is we're really doing here. Prophets try to tell us. We give each other pep talks. But in the end, it is our Father who will show us the true worth of our efforts and accept the offering that has made us most like Him.

He has honored that offering all along.

Exercise #3: Valuing Moms

Write down five things your mom has done to help you become the person you are today. Share the list with her if possible.

4

Taking the Train

An Exercise in Discovering Unexpected Blessings

It was a lovely autumn day. My college-age son and I left the house at the same time, he to go to school, I to work. As we approached our various cars, he said, "Uh-oh, Mom, looks like you've got a flat." It was true. And it was not just a little softening of the tire, the kind that requires a stop at the gas station for some air on the way to work. No, it was a full-on, sitting-on-the-rim flat tire, one that neither of us had the time to deal with at the moment.

"Come on, Mom," my son said. "I'm on my way to the TRAX station; you can just take the train in to town with me and then we'll fix your tire tonight." It seemed like a reasonable idea (being actually the only alternative that came readily to mind), so we hopped in his car and headed the two miles to the light-rail stop and got on a train.

Twenty minutes later, when I got off the train, I realized that I was much closer to my office than I would have been if I had taken my car to work. Parking in downtown Salt Lake City was a nightmare because of the massive construction taking place there, and I usually had a quarter-mile walk from the lot to which I had been assigned. It was only half a block from the TRAX stop to my building's front door. I had never been inclined to employ mass transit on a regular basis because I begrudged the time it added to my commute, but in the current circumstances it actually tacked on only a few minutes. And I knew that the ride home, when the freeways were always clogged with traffic, would likely be even closer to a wash, time-wise. So I marched up to Human Resources and signed myself up for a transit pass, and I began taking the train to work.

I soon learned that there were other benefits besides not having to park and walk. I almost always get a seat on the train. (I've got the little-old-lady thing going for me now, and there's usually a well-behaved college student whom I can guilt into a chivalrous gesture with a carefully placed glance.) I can read on my way to and from town, and in my line of work there is *always* something that needs reading, such that even if the ride adds a few minutes to my commuting time, the net effect is to give me more time working, not less.

Then winter came around, and I realized that I didn't feel my customary stomach-clenching panic when it snowed. If I could work my way the two little miles up to the train station, I was set—no fear of accidents, no white-knuckling it into town in heavy traffic, no two-hour waits to get around slide-offs and fender benders. I couldn't believe how much less stressful it was!

Winter became spring, and gas prices began to creep up, then to jump up, then to soar through the stratosphere. That was hard, but since I was only filling up my tank about once every three to four weeks, I barely felt it.

Sure, mass transit is not the solution for everyone, and it's not always ideal for me. In the morning, and again at the end of the workday, I find myself living in fifteen-minute increments. If I can't get out the door right on time for one train, I know I'll have to take the next one, so I sit back and get involved in something I think will take just a few minutes, and before I know it I've missed the next train as well. And sometimes I really miss being able to run errands on the way home from work. But by and large, it has been a real blessing to me that I had that long-ago flat tire and learned how to take the train.

This has alerted me to the possibility that there might be other blessings waiting around the corners of my life that I have not yet received because of my unwillingness to even try something different. I mean, the TRAX option was available to me for years before unforeseen circumstances pushed me to it. What else might be waiting out there that I don't even know about because I'm so caught up in my routine that I haven't looked for it?

I do know this much: The world is rich with resources and opportunities. If we shake things up every now and then, we might be surprised with what awaits us out there!

Exercise #4: Discovering Unexpected Blessings

Pick one thing in your life to do differently this week. Maybe it's taking an alternate form of transportation, or trying out that discount store you keep driving past, or experimenting with a new recipe, making something from scratch that you would usually buy "pre-fabbed." See if there are some unexpected blessings waiting for you when you shake up your life a little.

5

The Tax Return

An Exercise in Understanding Perspective

I was a crummy art student. Totally two-dimensional. I never did get the hang of those angled lines leading to the horizon point that were supposed to help us grasp the rules of perspective. I've accepted the fact that I have no visual skill, but at least intellectually I can understand that one building may seem smaller than another because it's farther away and not because it really is smaller. I get the notion that perspective has a lot to do with our perceptions of reality.

This is true in other areas of life besides art. For example, one year I was doing our tax return when I realized that our circumstances had shifted rather dramatically over the past couple of years and we hadn't been paying enough attention.

We had derived more income from unexpected, one-time channels than was customary for us. A couple of our dependents had grown up. Other children, though they were still dependents, had ceased to be eligible for the tax credits we had taken over the years.

What it amounted to, bottom line, was that we owed thousands of dollars in taxes. After I wiped the tears away and said a little prayer to try to calm the panic in my heart, I began assessing our resources, trying to figure out where we would get the money. I came up with about half of it but was at a loss as to where the rest might come from. We would probably have to borrow it from somewhere, which I hated doing, but I didn't see any other way.

My husband came home, and I was tearfully leafing through the forms to show him the bad news when I realized that I had calculated the tax we owed in the "Single" column instead of "Married, Filing Jointly." I quickly redid the numbers to discover that, although we still owed a pile of money, it was not more than we had on hand. It would be hard to quantify the relief I felt.

Here's the funny thing. If I had done the taxes right the first time, and seen the correct figure of what we owed, I would have been seriously bummed. It was a lot of money, after all. But because I *thought* we owed so much more, that exact same figure actually became a cause for rejoicing, a number filled with relief and celebration instead of depression and frustration.

That's the power of perspective.

How can we harness this power to help us feel happier? One principal key is simply in recognizing that it exists. When things are hard, or scary, or just plain annoying, the first thing I like to do is say, "Is this really as bad as it seems?" And, just as my thumbnail isn't really bigger than the moon (it's just closer), chances are that this challenge isn't really as big as it feels. It's just closer to my heart right now than other things.

I remember a time when I was having a real challenge toilet training one of my kids. This particular child, though not belligerent about the process, just couldn't be bothered. Our life was a constant series of dribbles. I was so frazzled anytime we went out in public, it was hardly worth leaving the house. I knew the location of every restroom in every grocery store and restaurant and library and shopping center within a twenty-mile radius of my house. It pretty much consumed my life.

One day when I was whining about this, my dad said to me, "Relax. Do you know anyone who goes to kindergarten in diapers?" It was as if someone had flipped a switch in my head and turned on the light, revealing how minor this problem really was and how soon, relatively speaking, it would be all in the past.

I don't mean to minimize our trials, though. Sometimes we experience things that truly *are* bad—really, really bad—and they will be for a long time. That's when we have to pull out the extra-wide-angle lenses and try to see our problems through the perspective of eternity. The solemn truth is this: "Earth has no sorrow that heav'n cannot heal" (*Hymns*, no. 115). Maybe it will take us our whole lives to feel that healing. Maybe we won't appreciate it fully on this side of the veil. But the Lord's promises are sure: "God shall wipe away all tears from their eyes; and there shall be no more death, neither sorrow, nor crying, neither shall there be any more pain" (Revelation 21:4).

Mortality exacts of every one of us more "penalties" than we are able to pay. We are subject to the consequences of our sins, our bad choices. We also make mistakes out of our weakness that aren't intentional sins but that still bear consequences. And we all know people who have suffered the consequences of the sins and mistakes made by others. Finally, many suffer innocently the effects of living in a world where things like tsunamis and hurricanes and typhus and smallpox happen.

It doesn't seem fair. From our limited perspective, in fact, it *isn't* fair. But is this really as bad as it seems?

What if we knew that Someone had paid in advance for all these difficulties?

What if we believed that they could all work together for our good? (See D&C 90:24; 122:7.)

What if we understood that the very things that drive us to our knees are putting us in the exact position to find our Heavenly Father and our Savior? What if, in turning us to heaven because we have nowhere else to go, our difficulties actually point the path to the salvation and exaltation we came to earth seeking in the first place? It's a different perspective, isn't it?

Just as I never mastered the perspective lines in art class, I will never (in this life, at least) fully understand God's perspective. But the light of the Son helps me trust that all is right, that an eternal perspective does indeed exist, and that one day all our problems will be in the past.

Exercise #5: Understanding Perspective

Pick a tree, or a building, or something else in the distance that you know is large. Close one eye and hold your thumb up to the open eye in such a way as to block that large item from your view. Is your thumb as big as a tree? Of course not, silly! Now think of some eternal blessing you hope one day to receive. Put all your mortal challenges between you and that blessing in your mind, and say to each trial, "You're no bigger than my thumb!" See how perspective works?

6

For Mrs. Silcox, Wherever You Are
An Exercise in Returning Thanks

I had been a student at the University of Utah for nearly a year. It was spring, and I was strolling across campus enjoying the fair day when a thought suddenly struck me, in a way I would describe as bewilderingly random: "You're in the wrong major."

I was an elementary education major at the time, the field I had settled on probably as early as junior high. I had always loved and been fascinated by children. I enjoyed working with them. It had never occurred to me to go in any other direction professionally.

But the unbidden thought had been so clear, and as I made room in my mind for it, it grew until it became unmistakable. I needed to change my major and, hence, my life's course. Regrettably, the prompting did not include direction as to what I should change my major *to,* so the pondering began. What did I love? Where might I fit in? Where could I be happiest?

As my mind flitted across various subjects, the light always seemed to be on over the one that read "English." I discarded that notion at first—as wrong as teaching elementary school had started to seem for me, the thought of teaching high school English was even worse. And what else was there to do with an English degree? But I couldn't deny that English was my absolute favorite subject, and I figured that Mrs. Silcox, my high school English teacher, must have had something to do with that.

Virginia Silcox taught Advanced Placement English at Skyline High School the year I was a senior there. I loved everything about her class, from the lively way she taught to the wild enthusiasm she felt for her subject. I will never forget the delight with which she would describe for us the scenes we were about to encounter in Charles Dickens's *The Pickwick Papers,* or the way she teared up when she was reading aloud Dylan Thomas's "Poem in October."

Mrs. Silcox didn't just read the papers we turned in; she commented on them, sometimes at length. She always made me feel like there were things she and I understood differently from the rest of the students in our class. One afternoon, she took great care explaining to us how to read a poem aloud, how not to turn the rhythm of a line into a singsong cadence or pound the rhyme at the end. Then she asked one of the guys in our class to read a poem, and he lurched along, hitting the syllables in a ta-DUM, ta-DUM pattern and emphasizing the rhyming words at the end of each line. I was in the act of rolling my eyes when I chanced to glance at Mrs. Silcox. She saw how annoyed I was and gave me a little smile and a wink that seemed to say, "I know, isn't it dreadful?" With that one look, she admitted me into the realm of people who "got it," and I felt a particular bond with her that makes me think of her fondly now, more than thirty years later.

So I took a deep breath and majored in English, not having the slightest idea what I would do with my degree, until I discovered as a senior that there were companies out there that might actually pay a person for obsessive spelling and grammatical correctness. And after I had spent several happy years as an editor, I thought I ought to try to find Mrs. Silcox and thank her. I wanted to thank her for loving English and for helping me to love it too. I wanted to tell her that a big portion of my current happiness could be traced back to my decision to change my major to English, a decision that had been influenced heavily by her teaching. I wanted her to know that her work had mattered in my life, that I counted her as one of my blessings.

Why does the hymn "Count Your Blessings" suggest that "it will surprise [us] what the Lord has done" (*Hymns,* no. 241)? Could it be that we lose track? I know there are times when I feel picked on or put upon or just plain grouchy, and they're usually the times when I forget what has been done for me, both by unnumbered people in this world and by unrecognized assistance from heaven.

I never found Mrs. Silcox. I tried contacting her through the school district's retirement office but hit a dead end, and I didn't know what else to do so I kind of dropped it. But not finding her has made me all the more determined to be on the alert for how people are affecting my life, or my children's lives, and to remember to thank them while I still can.

So, thanks, Mrs. Silcox, wherever you are. And thanks, Mr. Huntington, and Mrs. Tarrant, and Mr. Burley, and a whole host of teachers who see children as individuals and nurture their uniqueness and help them discover their competence. Thank you, youth leaders who show up prepared week after week even when a lot of times just one child comes to class. Thank you to the organist and chorister who led us in singing a hymn that answered a question my heart was asking. Thank you to the poet who wrote the words to that hymn, and to the people who put it in the hymnbook, and . . . you get the idea.

What you do matters. It does. We all have more influence than we dare to dream. Let's thank each other for it!

Exercise #6: Returning Thanks

Write a thank-you note (or even an e-mail) to someone this week. Tell the person specifically what he or she did that made a difference to you.

7

FatBoys

An Exercise in Understanding Men

My children are now all of the age where male-female relationships play a prominent role, and watching them has reminded me how mystified I was as a young adult woman at the seeming unfeelingness of the young men in my world. This extended into my married life, in which I could scarcely believe that my husband could be so clueless as to not recognize how it affected me when, for example, he didn't even care enough about our family to take out the garbage.

Now, many years later, I've seen the research studies that suggest men's brains are actually structured differently from women's brains, and that the connection between brain hemispheres that allows women to multitask and to process complex relationship issues is typically not as developed in men. Their brains are programmed to forge ahead single-mindedly and conquer problems—a significant and perhaps undervalued skill in today's culture.

A chance scene in volume 5 of the *Harry Potter* series illustrates these brain differences beautifully. In volume 4, Harry had a crush on a girl named Cho but could never get anywhere with her because she had a boyfriend. That boyfriend, Cedric, was killed by the evil wizard Voldemort in front of Harry's eyes at the end of volume 4. In volume 5, Cho and Harry end up in a situation where they kiss. It's the culmination of Harry's dream, but Cho is crying the whole time. Harry expresses his bewilderment over this to his friends Ron and Hermione, and Ron is as confused as Harry is. Not so with Hermione.

> Hermione looked at the pair of them with an almost pitying expression on her face.
>
> "Don't you understand how Cho's feeling at the moment?" she asked.
>
> "No," said Harry and Ron together.
>
> Hermione sighed and laid down her quill.
>
> "Well, obviously, she's feeling very sad, because of Cedric dying. Then I expect she's feeling confused because she liked Cedric and now she likes Harry, and she can't work out who she likes best. Then she'll be

feeling guilty, thinking it's an insult to Cedric's memory to be kissing Harry at all, and she'll be worrying about what everyone else might say about her if she starts going out with Harry. And she probably can't work out what her feelings toward Harry are anyway, because he was the one who was with Cedric when Cedric died, so that's all very mixed up and painful. Oh, and she's afraid she's going to be thrown off the Ravenclaw Quidditch team because she's been flying so badly."

A slightly stunned silence greeted the end of this speech, then Ron said, "One person can't feel all that at once, they'd explode." (Rowling, 459)

I laughed and laughed when I read that because it was such a brilliant example of the differences in how men and women see the world. And understanding that there *are* differences, and that those differences are fairly common, makes it easier not to be offended when men don't always seem to "get it."

To give the men in my life credit, I think they try. Take Mother's Day in my ward, for example. To start with, the men take over the Church jobs of all the women in the ward so that they can relax and attend Sunday School and Relief Society and be together. I think that's a great start, don't you?

Then, I know (because my husband has spent years in

various bishoprics) that they agonize over what gift to present to the mothers. Plants are a frequent choice, but we have many apartment dwellers in our ward who have no place to plant them. Cut flowers seem to be out of the question—too many men perceive them as a waste of money (although women in surveys say they would rather receive fresh flowers than a plant). One year we got a nice booklet. Another year I was in Seattle on Mother's Day, and the bishopric in that ward presented the women with large-size Cadbury chocolate bars, which I applaud most heartily except I know our bishopric shies away from those, too, as unsuitable for diabetics.

Next is the awkwardness of how to present the gift. It has long been the practice to include all the women, not just those who have borne children. The instinct is right, but it's still tough for the single women in our ward to make themselves stand up. And the day is tough for lots of mothers, too, who don't feel like they measure up to the "ideal mother" who is likely to be extolled in the sacrament meeting talks, so the bishopric sweats over whom to invite to give those talks as well.

They just don't want to offend anyone. That seems to be their primary goal on Mother's Day: It's not to honor the moms. It's not to honor motherhood or even womanhood in general. It's just to not make anyone upset. This is not their fault. This is *our* fault (the women's, I mean) for making it all complicated emotionally and for reading the wrong message into everything they're trying to do.

Contrast this with Father's Day. For many years, we didn't even observe Father's Day in our ward, and no one ever complained. (That should be a clue right there as to the differences between men and women.) Now we have a tradition that during the last ten minutes of priesthood meeting, they gather all the classes from deacons to high priests together in the multi-purpose room and present them with FatBoy ice-cream sandwiches. Everyone is happy. No one tries to probe for subliminal meaning in the choice of FatBoys. They eat their ice cream and yuk it up and go home happy.

What would happen in your ward if they tried to give FatBoys to the women on Mother's Day? Almost too horrible to contemplate, isn't it?

So, which is better, the men's way or the women's way? Neither, of course. They're just different. Instead of being frustrated by those differences, we can actually come to value them. I know I have grown to appreciate my husband's steady clarity when I've gotten emotionally overwrought about a situation. And he seems to appreciate my ability to "read" the children and understand what's going on in their brains that is affecting their actions. We need both skills in our family, and in our ward, and in our world.

Exercise #7: Understanding Men

The next time you're frustrated because you don't seem to be getting a response from the man in your life, remind yourself that he's not being deliberately obtuse. It's just the way he's wired. Communicate your needs clearly and directly, and don't forget to express gratitude when they are met.

8

One Big Cookie

An Exercise in Rethinking Assumptions

Here is the ridiculous and ineffective way in which I live my life: If I have treats within my reach, I eat them. Many is the large-economy-size package of Oreos or peanut M&Ms or some similar treat that I have purchased "for the kids" or "to last a week" or "because they're on sale" that I have ended up consuming single-handedly (or single-mouthedly, as the case may be) within twenty-four hours. I used to have the metabolism for that. No more. It wouldn't be hard for any reasonably astute person to pick me out of a lineup as the woman guilty of eating the whole sleeve of Pecan Sandies last night.

So I'm doing my best in this stage of my life to just avoid

buying the treats in the first place. I still crave them, I still often long for them, but if I don't have them right there, it's generally possible for me to resist the cravings. (Not always, mind you. But generally.)

However, I was at a daylong conference a couple of years ago and made the conscious, rational decision to have a treat with my lunch. In oh-so-reasonable fashion, I walked right past the Oreos, even though the slender box held only one row rather than the two that come in a whole package. I selected a single "big cookie" instead, knowing that I would consume in its entirety whatever I purchased, so the only way to limit myself to a reasonable number of calories was to buy just one item.

I ate the nutritious portion of my lunch and turned with anticipation to the cookie. Then, like an idiot, as I was unwrapping it, I started to read the nutrition information on the label. I think I just wanted to be vindicated in having bought that cookie instead of what I had really wanted, which was the box of Oreos. I scanned the tiny type until I found the line I was looking for: "Calories per serving: 160." Oh, good job!

Alas, I continued reading. "Servings per container: 4."

Are you kidding me? Who in her right mind invites her three closest friends to share her one cookie? It ain't *that* big, folks. I just can't tell you how disillusioned I was with the food industry for what seemed like an incredibly deceptive way to spin that nutrition info.

When I calmed down, it occurred to me that a person who insists on consuming large cookies probably deserves the letdown she gets if she's dumb enough to read the nutrition info on the package. If nutrition were really a concern, she wouldn't be buying the cookie in the first place. But it did seem as if I ought to be able to assume that one cookie would be intended to be fully consumed by one person.

This has caused me to reflect on the whole idea of the assumptions we sometimes make. They may seem logical at the time, but upon reflection many of them just don't hold up. For instance . . .

"No one likes me in this ward." On what evidence would you base that assumption? "Well, they never sit by me in Relief Society." Where do you sit? Are you always the first one there, and they file in around you and are careful to leave a wide berth? Or is it possible that you come in and sit alone instead of choosing a seat next to someone?

"I've blown my diet now; I might as well just give it up and eat what I want." Maybe you had a binge today. You really can start fresh tomorrow. You don't have to toss the whole plan just because it didn't work out perfectly today.

"I must not have really repented because I committed the same sin again. I guess I don't know what real repentance is." Repentance is as real as your heart is true at the time you're doing it. Often it takes multiple tries to forsake a sin completely. That doesn't mean your repentance wasn't sincere each time. It just means temptation is always there. Fortunately, so is the opportunity to repent when we succumb.

"I'm too old to skydive." Well, that one may be true. But if you really, truly wanted to skydive, I'll bet you could contrive a way to do it, regardless of your age. Former president George H. W. Bush did it to celebrate his 80th birthday, remember?

I'm just saying, if you look closely at some of your assumptions, they might turn out to be as ridiculous as the thought that you might split one cookie four ways. Try it and see.

Exercise #8: Rethinking Assumptions

The next time you catch yourself feeling badly about the way you've been treated, take a minute to check your assumptions. Maybe you've misinterpreted someone's actions or intentions. What would be different if you assumed instead that the person adored you and would be horrified to think he or she had upset you? Bonus exercise: Next time you're ready to give up on something because it's just too hard, rethink your assumptions. You may not be failing at all, just slowing in your forward progress for a bit. Keep trying!

9

Motherguilt, Part 1
An Exercise in Letting Go

Having been a mom for going on thirty years now, and having observed many, many other mothers in various stages of the work, I have come to believe that one of the most pervasive forces in the universe is Motherguilt—that nagging feeling that somehow everything that goes wrong in a family's life is the mother's fault.

For me, it started when I brought my first baby home from the hospital. I was trying (not altogether successfully) to nurse her, and every time she cried I thought, "Oh, no. What did I eat?" I never pursued that line of inquiry very far for fear that chocolate might be the culprit. (Any child born into my family is going to have chocolate as a way of life, and might as well get used to it.) But because she was just a tiny baby, I figured that if she was upset about something, it must be my fault, right?

I feel sorry for mothers nowadays who have the "benefit" of all this research that is being done about the effects of various forces on the unborn. Now, if your baby isn't gregarious and brilliant and delightful from day one, it's probably because you didn't play enough Mozart to the fetus *in utero.* You get to start feeling guilty even earlier than I did!

But I found that I experienced Motherguilt on a more personal level as well. I found myself wondering how I could recognize motherhood as the vital, exalted, noble calling I believed it to be when there were so many times when I found it tedious, repetitious, and not especially rewarding. Particularly, I remember bemoaning the fact that I had evidently spent four years in college to become the Candyland Champion of Atherton Drive. And then I felt guilty for feeling that way.

I was lucky enough to have a career that could be pursued largely off-site, so after I started having children, I was able to be home with them and still work professionally for at least a few hours a week. The challenge there was that, for a mother of young children, free time is rarely broken into chunks as large as an hour. Coming up with a few quiet hours a week for concentrated work is not as easy as it sounds. I discovered how well I was succeeding at this one day when I caught a snatch of my two-year-old's conversation with her doll: "Be *quiet!* Can't you see Mommy is trying to *work?*" I distinctly remember the feeling I often had that if I had hired a day-care provider to care for my children, and if she cared for them the way I was caring for them, I would fire her! It seemed like Walt Disney spent more time with my little ones than I did. And I felt guilty for that.

Then, when the youngest went to school, we decided I would go back to work full-time. It was the right decision for our family for many reasons, but the downside was that there never seemed to be enough of me to go around. And I felt guilty for that.

Where does this Motherguilt spring from in the first place? I'm not sure, but I don't think dads feel this way. Could our understanding of the crucial role of mothers, which ought to be so encouraging and ennobling, actually be partly to blame? I was raised on the maxim: "The mother sets the tone in the home." I think this is true, to an extent. Certainly its corollary—"If Mama ain't happy, ain't nobody happy"— seems accurate. But there is a problem with believing that as the mother you are the one who controls the atmosphere.

For example, I can get up early in the morning, chirpy as

a spring lark, ready to make the perfect breakfast for my family, going into their rooms to awaken them with a song. One child will wake up grumpy—for no discernible reason. And all my determined efforts to ungrump that child will be in vain. He'll start poking his sister, and stealing bites of waffle off her plate, and pretty soon she's crying and the boys are hitting each other and I'm over in the corner desperately singing "Let Us Oft Speak Kind Words to Each Other" and wondering how things got out of control so fast. Now, did I set that tone in my home?

There's a scripture in the Book of Mormon that has become one of my "unfavorite" verses: "Therefore, cheer up your hearts, and remember that ye are free to act for yourselves—to choose the way of everlasting death or the way of eternal life" (2 Nephi 10:23). I used to like that scripture until I realized that it applied to my children as well. Sometimes it's just plain hard to live with a whole houseful of little free agents, and believing that you control the tone in that home can be an exercise in frustration.

Another challenge with this is that you don't always get to control a child's environment. We decided early on not to buy toy guns for our boys because in theory we didn't want to encourage violent play. But what happened in actual practice was that a stick became a gun. A banana became a gun.

A finger became a gun. We finally broke down and bought the water pistols so that a banana could just be a banana again!

Plus, you don't get to control your children's reaction to the environment you *do* try to provide. I learned this by having multiple children. Thinking I had everything figured out by the time the second one came along, I was astonished to learn that the same stimuli did not necessarily evoke the same response in that second child. Or the third, or the fourth, or the fifth. I had one child for whom the mere suggestion of a reprimand was enough to have her in remorseful tears. She had a brother who would respond to an actual spanking with a defiant look that implied, "Is that all you got?" That wasn't something we had any control over—it was just the way those children *came.*

One of our boys was a somewhat timid, not-very-aggressive child. Per the custom of our generation, we enrolled him in soccer, but he never really got his foot on the ball. He seemed to be in it mostly for the uniform, with the bonus being snacking on the oranges at halftime. But one day, when our team was way ahead, the coach (who was a mom) pulled all the more aggressive little boys out of the game or into the backfield, leaving the quieter kids to take the lead. Suddenly, I found myself in the unaccustomed position of seeing my own son kicking the ball down the field! I was so excited for him! I ran along the sidelines, yelling, "Go for it! Yay!" He stopped in mid-stride, planted his hands on his hips, stomped over to the sideline, and hissed, "Stop *yelling* at me!" Apparently one child's praise is another child's pressure. How can you control something like that?

You can't.

Now, here's an important question to consider: When it snows in May, do you feel guilty? Frustrated, maybe; tired of snow and ready for winter to be over, maybe; but do you feel *guilty?* Of course not.

Why not?

Because you don't control the weather. And it would be silly and counterproductive to assume guilt for something you had no control over in the first place.

Now, read back over this chapter and consider all the things about your children that you just can't control, and ask yourself if maybe, just maybe, you've been carrying around some unnecessary guilt. You might get frustrated, you might feel tired, but it's counterproductive to assume *guilt* for something you had no control over in the first place. Recognizing that simple fact about life is the first step in learning to let go of Motherguilt. And when you shed the guilt, somehow the frustration and the fatigue become more manageable, and you start to recognize the joy that is intended to be the greatest gift of being a mother.

Exercise #9: Letting Go

On a piece of paper, list everything that's driving you crazy about your kids right now. Then go down the list and for each item ask yourself, "Do I truly have any control over this?" If the answer is no, cross it off. Then let go of worrying about those things or feeling guilty about them, and focus your emotional energy on the items that remain on the list.

10

Motherguilt, Part 2

An Exercise in Taking Control

In Part 1 of our exploration of the phenomenon I call Motherguilt, we looked at a bunch of things that we don't control when we're raising a family. We can't control our children's moods. We don't have perfect control over their environment. We certainly don't control how they react to that environment. So what *can* we control?

Ourselves.

Admittedly, it's not always easy to exercise self-control, especially when a child seems determined to push all our buttons. But you can't have a fight unless both parties come out swinging. As parents, we can refuse to engage, and it's surprising how quickly troubles dissipate when we're not taking part in escalating them. For example, when my preteen daughter used to stomp off to her room shouting, "I hate you!" I liked to call cheerfully after her, "I know, but that will never alter my undying love for you." (It drove her crazy. That may have been part of why I did it.)

Sometimes I have to breathe deeply and instruct myself, "Be the parent. You are the adult here. It won't help the situation if you descend to the two-year-old's level."

The problem is, I'm only human. As much as I'd like to be in perfect control of my emotions, the sad truth is that sometimes I yell at my kids. Sometimes I say things I'm not so proud of. I remember one day when I spent a couple of hours crafting a salad for a potluck luncheon. As we were hurrying out the door, I dropped the bowl, scattering the morning's work across the floor. And I said a naughty word. It wasn't even the mildest naughty word I know.

In such a circumstance, when I have lost control, there's only one way for me to get it back. I have to repent! I apologize. I admit to my children that I too am subject to mistakes but that I'm going to try to do better. I often tell my children that I am giving them the gift of an imperfect mother so that they won't enter married life with any unrealistic expectations. (They generally just roll their eyes.)

I'm not happy with the fact that I mess up pretty

regularly. But now that I recognize that weakness, I can make a conscious effort to approach things differently. I'm getting better at biting my tongue, at removing myself from a toxic situation until it calms down, at being alert to potential danger points (hunger, fatigue) and trying to address them before they get out of hand. My self-control has improved over the years, but I still fall short.

The thing is, though, when we as parents admit our own mistakes, it helps our children see that making mistakes is just part of life, and that we can get past our mistakes and love each other even in our imperfections. It signals that we all have to keep trying every day to be better, even parents. And it gives our children the opportunity to forgive us, a Christlike act that can form a special bond.

So, we can start by working to control ourselves. Then, although we might not be able to control our children's environment perfectly, we can have some control over what *we* contribute. Maybe we can't make them sit still and listen during family home evening, but we can at least hold it. They might fall asleep during family prayer, but over time they'll learn how to seek the Lord when they need Him. My two-year-old granddaughter was sick with a cold once, and her mom heard her coughing in her room at night and went to check on her. She was all huddled up at the bottom of her bed, singing quietly to herself, "There is beauty all around [cough, cough], When there's love at home . . ." (*Hymns,* no. 294). When a tiny child who isn't feeling so well soothes herself in the night with "Love at Home," something really right is going on in that child's environment.

I have learned not to feel guilty for imperfection as long as I know I'm making a conscious effort to progress. I realized the value of this effort when our two youngest children were scheduled to receive their patriarchal blessings on the same day. That morning, the stake patriarch called me and said, "I'd like to come to your house to give those blessings, if it's all right with you." I agreed, hung up the phone, and started shouting "All hands on deck" to try to get the house in order. We couldn't have the patriarch sticking to our floor as he walked across it! And the stack of last night's pizza boxes didn't seem too conducive to the Spirit. It was a challenge, but we got things in order in time, and both blessings were just beautiful.

The patriarch turned to me afterward and said quietly, "I don't always do it this way, but I knew it would be safe to come to your home. I knew the Spirit could be here."

I can't tell you how good it made me feel to know that even in a home where the mom has to be repenting all the time, where occasionally an inappropriate word is spoken, where it might take five adults quite a bit of scrambling to make the place presentable—even there, when we're trying to have our hearts right, the Spirit can be present.

And when the Spirit is here, it never makes me feel guilty. It just makes me determined to keep trying, keep moving forward, and keep seeking the help I need to somehow get it right!

Exercise #10: Taking Control

If you've done something you're not proud of during an out-of-control moment, make a concrete plan for what you can do differently next time. Then go apologize to your kids and let them feel the joy of forgiving you.

11

Sluggish Luggage
An Exercise in Living Optimistically

I was traveling with a group of people to Alaska for a conference, and for once I got to the airport in plenty of time to check my bag if I wanted to. Usually I'm dashing so fast that it isn't even an option, but this time I had the luxury of choice.

That luxury is overrated, I think, because I was having a terrible time making up my mind what to do. We had a stopover in Seattle, and I hated dragging a bag through the airport, looking for the new gate for the next leg of the flight, and having to mind it while trying to eat lunch, and so on. On the other hand, I also hated the thought of making people wait for my checked bag. In the end, I decided I couldn't possibly be the only person in our group who would be checking a bag, so I handed it over.

When I met my friends at the gate, it turned out that yes, I actually *was* the only person to have checked a bag. I was a little frustrated about that, but oh well, that's how it goes sometimes. Could be worse.

It got worse. Right away. The people at the check-in desk called two of our party over on the intercom. The two came back a few minutes later, grinning. It turned out that the flight had been overbooked, and they were being asked to bump to a flight that left slightly later but got in earlier because it was a direct flight. They said they would be happy to be bumped if their friends could be bumped as well, so now all of a sudden we were all on a new, nonstop flight to Alaska.

"Did anyone check a bag?" the travel attendants asked as they created new boarding passes for us. Sheepishly I raised my hand. They got a description of my little suitcase and said they would do their best to get it onto the flight.

Well, you can imagine what happened. We got to Anchorage without incident, but my bag did not. It apparently hadn't gotten switched. There were the nice people waiting to take us home from the airport, and I had no suitcase. I offered to take a cab, but they insisted on taking us all to the hotel to get settled, then graciously shuttled me back to the airport an hour later for my luggage.

Fortunately, the airport was only about a fifteen-minute drive from the center of town, and my bag was waiting on the carousel when we walked in the door, so it wasn't nearly the hassle it might have been in another location. I thanked my drivers profusely, we went back to the hotel, and the conference was carried off without further complications.

I thought long and hard about this experience on the airplane ride home a couple of days later. At first I was upset that I had made a choice that subsequently proved itself to be a bad one in so many ways. But then I wondered. Yes, it had been a nuisance, but the problem had been easily remedied. It was a minor inconvenience, not a major catastrophe, as it easily could have become if the airport had been farther from town or if the flights had been separated by a longer time or—perish the thought—if the baggage handlers had gotten my luggage off the first flight but not gotten it onto the second one.

One thing I knew for certain: I would never again agonize over whether to check a bag that could be carried on. And I have since wondered if maybe that experience, with the decision that grew out of it, has saved me or may someday save me from a much worse trial.

It's just something to think about when life's little

annoyances flare up. What if we simply decided to believe that some of those things we're going through might end up shielding us from worse disasters? Maybe catching our kid skipping class rang some warning bells that encouraged us to step up our parenting a notch before he got into serious trouble. Maybe the car breaking down a week before the family vacation allowed us to have it towed from our driveway instead of the Nevada desert. Maybe my son's missing his flight on Christmas Eve made it possible for a standby passenger to get home to his wife and kids.

This is what living optimistically means to me. When I assume that even my frustrations serve a purpose, I'm able to get over them a lot more quickly. Sometimes they even make me smile when I can come up with a particularly ludicrous explanation for how they might be serving me. The main point is, we don't always get to choose what happens to us, but we always get to choose how we feel about it. That's a great power to have.

Exercise #11: Living Optimistically

The next time you encounter some nuisance or frustration, ask yourself, "How might this be helping me?" If it makes it any easier, turn to an imaginary friend and say, "Pollyanna, what do you think?" Be totally unrealistic if that's what it takes to free you up to laugh instead of fret.

12

The Engine-Free Car
An Exercise in Adjusting Expectations

In one of my all-time favorite classic *Candid Camera* episodes, the crew scouts out a location where a service station sits at the bottom of an incline. They position at the top of the hill a car from which the engine has been removed. They put Fannie Flagg, who plays a ditzy redhead, in the car, give it a push, and have her coast it into the station. This was in the days of full-service gas stations, you understand, and the attendant runs out and fills the car with gas, and then she sweetly asks him to check the oil. "It's been running a little rough," she explains.

Obligingly, the attendant goes to the front of the car and lifts the hood. The look on his face when he can't find the engine is priceless. He walks around to the back. Nope, not there, either. He's really perplexed now, and it is hilarious. Even funnier is the dialogue that ensues as he tries to explain the problem to the driver and she pretends to have no idea what he's talking about. "Well, for heaven's sake," she finally says, "I got the car *here,* didn't I?" And of course he has to admit that she did, but that it's going to be impossible for her to get it anywhere else.

"I don't understand," she insists. "Can't you just put another quart of oil in it?"

"Lady," he says, "a quart of oil ain't going to be enough to make this car run."

"Well, if you can't fix it, can you maybe refer me to someone who can? I'll just take it there."

And she strings him along for as long as she can. We're watching his blood pressure rise by the second. We're watching the internal war between his innate customer-is-always-right instincts and the impossible reality that sits in front of his face.

We laugh our heads off whenever we watch this clip. But one of the things that makes it funny—and even a bit painful—is that it is so true to the way we live our lives. How often do we insist that someone make the car run, even when we know in our hearts that the car has no engine?

This behavior takes many forms. We take an energetic two-year-old to the movies and insist that she sit quietly for two hours, then get mad when she can't. We spend all our money and then insist on buying more things even when we can't imagine how we'll pay for them. We fill our bodies with junk food and deprive them of sleep, and then get upset when they don't run properly. We're like Alma's son Corianton, who had to be told plainly, "Wickedness never was happiness," as much as he would have liked it to be otherwise (Alma 41:10).

When our expectations are clearly unrealistic, we have two choices: live in denial and find ourselves unhappy at every turn, or adjust those expectations.

In my young adult years, I saw a movie that had a profound effect on me. It was titled *The Other Side of the Mountain,* and it was based on the true story of national champion skier Jill Kinmont, who suffered an accident that paralyzed her from the neck down. She made it clear that she intended to walk again, and told her doctors that if they said she wouldn't, she was going to make them look silly.

The scene I remember most vividly is one in which she invites her fiancé to come to the hospital, finally ready for him to see the progress she has made in her recovery. He comes into the room holding a wrapped gift in his hand. She is seated in a chair, a bowl of potato chips in her lap. She tells him she's going to show him something amazing. Anticipation is high. With tremendous effort, she thunks her hand down into the bowl of chips and moves it around until she is able to get a chip in her grasp, then maneuvers the chip up to her mouth and eats it. "Ta-da!" she exclaims.

"Is that it?" he asks incredulously.

"Is that *it?* That's the hardest thing of all," she tells him.

"I thought you were going to walk for me. Aren't you going to walk?"

An expression of extreme sadness crosses her face. "No," she says flatly. "I'm never going to walk again."

He can't handle this news, and he rushes out of the room, leaving the present behind. She opens the box, which contains a new pair of ski boots. (When you're a young woman, this is where you start crying.)

So Jill Kinmont left her old life, her old plans, her old love behind. She went on to live a happy and productive life as a quadriplegic, but if she had insisted on clinging to her earlier expectations, she would have been miserable. It would have been like holding on to that engine-free car, insisting that someone *had* to make it run.

I have a dear friend who suffered a severe heart attack and ultimately had to have a heart transplant. During his long recovery process, his wife told me, "We are learning to live with a new normal." This was their way of expressing the adjustment they had made to their expectations. If they clung to the idea that everything would go back to the way it had been before his illness, they would have been disappointed. Things were not going to be "normal," in that sense, ever again. But instead of being perpetually sad at having lost their normal life, they chose to redefine that life with a new set of expectations as to what "normal" would look like. And I believe they have been happier than they ever thought they would be.

I'm not suggesting that we settle for mediocrity. It's great to have dreams. Indeed, one of the characteristics of charity is that it "hopeth all things" (1 Corinthians 13:7). But it's a great gift to be able to accept the realities of our lives and then to be able to work within those realities to soar higher than we would have imagined we could. We may find that the "new normal" is even better than the old one.

Exercise #12: Adjusting Expectations

Take an honest inventory of your life situation. Are you holding on to unproductive behaviors with the unrealistic expectation that they won't really hurt you? Is it time to reach for a "new normal," maybe even on a higher level?

13

Two Speeding Tickets
An Exercise in Making Lasting Changes

We have lived in the same house for going on thirty years now. And no, I'm sad to report that we're actually nowhere near the end of our mortgage, but we had a great addition built that will enable us to die in this house, so we're closer to being out of debt than we might have been if we'd had to move. But I digress. What I wanted to say was that, having lived here for roughly three decades, I estimate I have made the same turn off of 4700 South (a 50-mile-per-hour, four-lane highway) into our subdivision thousands of times. It's about three-tenths of a mile to our house from that turn, and I could probably drive it with my eyes closed.

So I was basically on autopilot one evening after work a

couple of summers ago, and I didn't see the speed trap that a policeman had laid behind a hedge in the driveway of one of the businesses along that short stretch of road. Sure enough, he came roaring after me, lights blazing, to inform me that I was going 36 miles per hour in a 25 miles per hour zone, and he gave me a ticket that ended up costing me $87.

Now, I'm pretty sure I wasn't being reckless. I don't think I was going any faster than I typically drive on my street. But the speed limit was clearly posted, and I had clearly exceeded it, so I took my lumps and my ticket and went home.

Exactly two weeks later, in exactly the same spot, I got pulled over again by that exact same policeman. I had been trying to be more cautious in that area, but on this particular night my mind was full of work problems and the book group I was hosting in a couple of hours and the packing I needed to do before going out of town the next day, and I had forgotten to pay attention. It was the last drop of stress I could handle, and when the policeman came to my window to ask for my license and registration, I was crying. Hard.

"You were going 36 miles per hour," he said. "This is a 25 mile per hour area."

"I know it is," I sobbed. "I'm so sorry."

He gave me the ticket anyway. So much for the myth that

a woman can cry herself out of getting a ticket. Maybe you have to be a much younger, cuter woman for that to work.

Well, it was obvious what was going on. I had developed, over many long years, the habit of driving that stretch of road at a certain speed—36 miles per hour, to be precise. And unless I wanted to pay $43.50 a week for that privilege (at least until they revoked my driver's license for excess points on my record), I needed to change that habit.

Fast-forward a year and a half, to a day when I was driving through our subdivision with my daughter on the way home from a party, and she commented, "Look at you, staying right within the speed limit. I'm proud of you, Mom!"

And I hadn't even been paying attention.

This incident gives me great hope. Clearly, if properly motivated, I can make a change in my life that lasts. The question now becomes, what would be sufficient motivation for me to make such changes in other areas of my life?

Will I have to be diagnosed with Type 2 diabetes in order to have the strength to kick my sugar habit? Will it take a heart attack to make me lose weight? How many late fees will be required to jolt me into remembering to pay my bills on time?

I *have* figured out how to be a much better housekeeper. Invite someone over every week. Doesn't have to be the same someone; just be sure an outsider is going to step through that door at least once in the course of the week, and see how easy it is all of a sudden to get that pile of dishes out of the sink.

Another thing I know is that the Spirit invites change. Most of the meaningful changes I've been able to make in the course of my life have been helped along by the nudging, the help, and the encouragement of the Spirit. So maybe the biggest change I should be making is to work harder to always have the Spirit. Maybe that's the motivation I've been looking for!

Exercise #13: Making Lasting Changes

Choose one small thing you want to change about your life. Don't pick a full-on diet, for example, but maybe just one eating habit you could alter. We're starting small on purpose so we can feel some success. Pray and ask for the Spirit to help you make that change. Write down all the reasons why you should make it, and why you can. Decide what motivators would help you stick to it. And then take a deep breath and do it!

14

Late Again

An Exercise in Suspending Judgment

My daughter and her husband are lovely, responsible, caring, service-oriented, faithful people. And they are chronically late. It is often a source of frustration, to them as well as to others, that they can't seem to get places on time.

I have a theory as to why this is so. I think most chronically late people have a totally unrealistic idea of how much time things take. So they commit themselves to too many things, too many people, too many activities, and they never seem to be able to squeeze them all in on time. It's not that they're being deliberately inconsiderate or that they don't care about other people's schedules or that they think they're more important than anyone else. They just genuinely don't know where the time goes.

These kids of mine lived in Rexburg for a while, and one weekend when I was giving a talk in Idaho Falls I invited them to make the half-hour drive to come to the conference I was participating in. Recognizing this challenge they have, I addressed it up front in no uncertain terms.

"This event starts at 9:00 AM *sharp*," I said, "and I really, really need you to be on time. I have seats for you up front with me. It would be very awkward to have you wander in late. It would make me really nervous to be wondering where you were. I want you to come, but it isn't possible for me to stress too much how vital it is that you get there on time."

They promised. Solemnly. And I believed I had put enough fear into their hearts to make it happen.

The next day dawned, and I got to the conference early for the prayer meeting and final briefing. I came out to my seat in the audience at about five minutes before 9:00. And my kids weren't there. The event began. And my kids weren't there. The producer ran through all the announcements, we had an opening song, and the first speaker started into her message. And my kids weren't there.

Oh, was I mad! I couldn't believe, after all I had done to impress upon them the *absolute need* to be on time, that they would let me down like this. It was going to be awful to have them waltz in late. My producers were going to think they were so rude. It would be distracting to the presenter. I sat there seething.

Then, to top it all off, my husband suddenly leapt up from his chair and walked out of the auditorium! *GREAT!* I have a whole family that can't behave in public! I wanted to shrink into the seat and just die.

My husband came back about five minutes later and sat down beside me again. He leaned over and whispered, "That was the kids, calling me on my cell." (He'd had it on silent; I didn't even know it had gone off.) "They've been in an accident. That's why they're not here yet." Seeing the stricken look on my face, he hastened to add, "They're okay, don't worry. It's just a fender bender, right outside. It wasn't their fault. Someone was hurrying to get to the event and clipped them trying to turn into the parking lot."

All of the judgments that had been rolling in my head now poured in and scalded my heart. I couldn't believe I hadn't given them the benefit of the doubt. I should have assumed that something unforeseen had happened to make it impossible for them to keep their promise. How awful would it have been if they'd gotten hurt! I was so thankful they were okay, and so ashamed that I had leapt to conclusions.

I learned an important lesson that day: The scriptures mean it when they say "Judge not." The truth is, we never have *all* the facts. We can never see what might have happened last night or last week or last year to make someone behave the way they do today. From our limited mortal perspective, the chance that we'll judge wrongly is astronomical. Thank goodness Heavenly Father doesn't leave it up to us!

Exercise #14: Suspending Judgment

The next time you're tempted to judge someone, stop and think instead, "What could I do to help?" Then do it, and be glad you're in a position to be so strong.

15

The Same Old Hymn
An Exercise in Hearing

I used to be stressed out about money pretty much all the time. I didn't really think of us as poor, although one year when I did the calculation just out of curiosity I realized we could have qualified for reduced-price lunches at the elementary school. (It was moot, because I couldn't get my kids to eat the elementary school lunches at any price.)

Somehow we've managed to squeak by, raising five kids, and we've had everything we needed and a good deal of what we wanted in all the thirty years of our marriage. We've seen lots of miracles in the course of it, money seemingly dropping out of nowhere when we've had unexpected expenses. For example, when I was pregnant with child number four, my husband changed jobs a few months before the baby was born, and to retain the insurance benefits, we had to pay the entire premium ourselves. It was a couple thousand dollars, all told—less, certainly, than the hospital expenses would have been without the insurance, but more than our little budget could really stand.

One day when I was fretting about this, I got a call from some random publishing company in California. They had gotten my name from a woman I used to do some freelance work for, a woman whom I hadn't talked to in several years. They had heard that I was trained in indexing, and they needed an index for a book right away. Could I do it? The California wage they were offering seemed immense, and I leapt on it. The amount they paid me was almost enough to cover the entire extra expense of having that child. And they never called me again.

We've seen many similar miracles, including the orchestration of our professional lives to the extent that when our two oldest children received their mission calls on the same day, we were able to say with confidence that we could support them both financially in the field. It was a blessing we could not have imagined even five years earlier.

So I thought I had reached the point where I wasn't really going to worry about money anymore. Then we had a big, totally unexpected financial burden drop on us, and I felt that familiar sense of semi-panic wash through me. What could we do? Where might that extra cash come from? Why did I always have to be dealing with this kind of thing?

That Sunday, for the opening hymn in sacrament meeting, we sang, "We Thank Thee, O God, for a Prophet" (*Hymns,* no. 19). If ever there was a hymn I could sing in my sleep, it would be that one. It's so very familiar that I usually drone through it without really thinking about the words. But this time, as we were trundling along through the verses, a line just reached out and grabbed me by the heart. It was this one: "We doubt not the Lord nor his goodness. We've proved him in days that are past."

Was that not so? the Spirit whispered to me. Had I not seen the hand of the Lord in preserving us financially in times when I had absolutely no idea of how that would be possible? Why would I think that He would abandon us now?

My heart soared. It was the message I needed most at that time, delivered in so ordinary and even mundane a fashion that I might easily have missed it. I was so grateful I had gotten to sacrament meeting in time for the opening hymn, so grateful that the Spirit had been with us in the meeting and able to nudge me to pay attention, so grateful to William

Fowler for writing the words in the 1800s that would contain exactly the message I would need in the 2000s.

That experience has made me much more keenly aware of how important it can be to just "show up" for life. The scriptures tell us that "all things denote there is a God" (Alma 30:44), but we have to open our eyes to see Him. He speaks to us in so many different ways:

The words of hymns, of scripture, of poetry, of good books have often impressed themselves on my mind in life-changing ways.

I have seen Him send people into my life who have been uniquely positioned to help me with the struggles I was experiencing at that particular season.

When I have gone to meetings or listened to general conference with my heart open and my pen and paper in hand, I have frequently heard something that seemed aimed directly at me.

Another "same old hymn" holds an important key for me in remembering to trust the Lord. The line I'm thinking of goes like this: "Count your many blessings; name them one by one, And it will *surprise* you what the Lord has done" (*Hymns,* no. 241; emphasis added). Isn't it odd that, after all these years and all these evidences, I would still be *surprised* to realize what the Lord has done for me? I wish that weren't so, but it seems to be. The increasingly rapid sweeping by of time makes me forgetful.

That's why I'm grateful for the "same old hymns." When things get turbulent, the words that have long since lodged in my mind and heart can be brought to remembrance by the Spirit, and I can see clearly all the wonderful surprises the Lord has given me.

Exercise #15: Hearing

Get to sacrament meeting a little early one week. Look up the hymns that you'll be singing that day, and read through the words carefully and prayerfully. Is there a special message for you there?

16

Clueless in Seattle

An Exercise in Acknowledging Limitations

A few years ago, we went through a major, company-wide training program at work. It started at the executive level, filtered down to some of the senior employees, and from there needed additional helpers to spread it throughout the company. I was selected to be one of the teachers of these concepts, and I was excited and felt pretty important to be asked to go to Seattle and St. George to share the training with store associates there.

I was especially excited to be going to Seattle, where I had some good friends I could stay with, and I looked forward to that event for weeks. Unfortunately, the week before I was to leave, I came down with a whopper of a cold. It was one of those viruses that just settles in and shows no sign of leaving—the cough, the clogged-up head, the slowness of brain and motion that makes you feel as if you're swimming in a pot of some particularly dense soup.

But I wanted desperately to go to Seattle, so I persuaded myself that it was "no big deal" and that I could medicate the symptoms and be just fine. Armed with the strongest over-the-counter medications money could buy, I got on the plane and headed out.

About midway through the plane ride, I realized I didn't have in my carry-on tote the binder of training materials I had brought with me. I looked all around me and under the seats. Nothing. I checked the overhead compartment. Not there. By now I was seriously panicked. Not only did I need that notebook to execute the training, but the material in it was confidential and proprietary. I could get in big trouble if someone else got hold of it.

I spent the second half of the flight in a cold sweat, running through the events of that morning over and over in my mind. I had had the notebook when I left home; I could remember thumbing through it in the terminal when I was waiting for the flight to be called. Had I left it there? Probably. Could I get it back? Maybe, but not in time to do me any good in Seattle. I got out some index cards I had with me and started trying to reconstruct everything I could remember about the training so I could at least give the associates some idea of what it was all about. And I prayed.

"Please don't let the wrong person get hold of that notebook," I begged. "Please let it just be turned in to the airline, so I can pick it up on my way home and no one will be the wiser. Please take into account how crummy I feel, and cover me for this awful mistake."

The plane landed. I collected my bag from the overhead bin and was starting down the aisle when I saw the notebook sitting in an empty seat two rows in front of me. My mind was suddenly clear for a moment, and I could picture myself setting it down on that seat as I rearranged things to fit into the overhead compartment. The flight wasn't full; my training notebook had evidently sat there untouched the whole time. I grabbed it up and hugged it to me, almost weeping with the tangible feeling of relief.

The drama of it all, coupled with the drinks on the flight, combined to make me seek urgently for a restroom as soon as I hit the terminal. I went in, got freshened up and calmed down, and then worked my way down the long, long concourse to meet my friends. We were loading my things in the back of their car when I looked around and realized . . . I didn't have the notebook. After all that agony, after the despair of thinking it was lost and the euphoria of finding it intact, I had left it behind yet again! This time, I could picture clearly where I had propped it up on the sink in the restroom as I washed my hands.

I dashed back into the terminal, but of course, they don't just let you down the concourse in the airport without a boarding pass. I had to weasel my way in front of a bunch of people in line at the airline customer service desk to tell them my problem. They gave me a "dummy" permit and walked me through security, and I dashed down the hall to the restroom at the very end of that ridiculously long concourse and burst through the door and there it was, just where I had left it. I scooped up the notebook, ran back to my friends, turned in the dummy badge, and collapsed into the car.

It might be superfluous to say at this point that the training was not quite what it might have been under happier circumstances.

What on earth had happened? The explanation was quite simple, really: I was sick. I wasn't well enough to be operating on all cylinders, and so I made stupid mistakes and had trouble concentrating even on a really important thing like not losing the notebook that was my reason for being in Seattle in the first place. We got through the training all right, and I felt like the Lord compensated for my lack of effectiveness so that others wouldn't suffer the consequences of my personal inadequacy (He does that quite often, I've found), but it all would have been so much better if I had just been willing to call the Seattle store manager and say, "Hey, I'm not feeling up to this. Can we please reschedule your training, or maybe send one of the other teachers up to help you instead?"

In fact, I did that very thing with the St. George store manager the minute I got home from Seattle. Yes, I had to swallow some pride to ask him to push the training back a few weeks, and I hated to inconvenience him in that way, but he was happy to accommodate me. We ended up having a much better experience than we had had in Seattle, much more in line with what those people needed.

Oh, pride. That foolish, foolish little quality that makes it so hard for us to admit that we need help, that we can't do everything all the time, that we might have limitations. Whenever I have succumbed to its subtle, seductive call, I have been the loser for it. I have made things worse that I was trying to make better. I have deprived others of opportunities to serve. I have looked silly, made messes that someone else had to clean up, and botched tasks that could have been done with ease if I had let others help with them from the outset.

I'm not advocating "learned helplessness," that little trick of the children that gets them out of doing the laundry because they keep forgetting to put the soap in. I think we *should* stretch, and try things that are outside our customary level of expertise, and always be striving to grow and get better.

However, I believe there are times when we know darn well that we shouldn't be saying yes to a task. But pride gets in the way, and we tell ourselves we want to help when really we just don't want to admit that we don't have the resources— time or money or skill or physical stamina or whatever—to do our best.

I know I've said this before, but it bears repeating as one of the important lessons I've learned and relearned many times in my life:

If you say yes when your heart is saying no, nobody wins.

Chances are, you'll feel resentful and frazzled and end up doing more harm than good to your relationship with the person you were trying to please in the first place. That's a no-win. And the person who made the assignment doesn't win either if you can't carry it out properly.

Take it from me: You don't want to end up clueless in Seattle, running down the endless concourses of life searching for your lost notebook. If you need help, ask for it. If you're not in a position to help, ask to be excused. Recognize that, although there are plenty of times when the Lord grants us strength beyond our own, there are other times when He expects us to be good stewards of our resources and to learn how to apportion them wisely. Learn to discern the difference so that you *can* be there when He really needs you.

Exercise #16: Acknowledging Limitations

If you're feeling overburdened, prayerfully choose one activity this week to say no to. Then skip that activity without feeling guilty, without feeling like you have to explain, without worrying about what others will think. See—was that so hard?

CHAPTER

17

Unsightly Sock Lines
An Exercise in Keeping It Real

I once made the strategic error of getting on a plane without a book to read. Resorting to the magazines in the seat pocket in front of me, I pulled out a copy of the Sky Mall catalog. I was soon engrossed in descriptions of products I had never imagined existed. One headline in particular caught my eye: "Now Unsightly Sock Lines Can Be a Thing of the Past."

This was intriguing to me. I wasn't even sure what an "unsightly sock line" was. In my world, it would probably have been defined as the spot where the tops of my knee-high hose failed to meet up with the hem of the dress I was wearing.

Not so. Apparently some people are careless enough to spend extended time in the sunshine with ankle socks on. When the socks are removed, the point where the tan ends is an unsightly sock line. Fortunately, there is a remedy. For something in the neighborhood of two hundred dollars, you can purchase the Tootsie Tanner, a sunlamp designed specifically for the feet. You can smooth out your tan while relaxing, reading a book, or watching TV.

This seems problematic to me. Tans are tricky things. What happens if you overbake your feet—back on with the socks and out into the sunshine once more? What if you don't calculate the border just right, and you end up with an overlapping area with a darker stripe? Hey—if your tan was so important to you, why did you wear ankle socks outside in the first place?

Maybe, if they wanted to call that device a Tootsie *Warmer,* I could buy into the concept. My feet are always cold, even with those cozy slipper socks that are so readily available these days, the ones with the non-slip spots all over the bottom that make it feel like you're walking on Legos when you cross the kitchen floor. A heat lamp might be my answer, but I don't think I'm willing to shell out $199.99 even for toasty toes. In the end, the whole thing is just kind of bizarre.

Here's a different headline that promises a really useful benefit, though: "Dine with Children Worry-Free." Now, *that* is a product I must have. What magic have the manufacturers wrought? Tip-proof milk glasses? Safety belts to keep the children in place until they've finished their peas? A sound-proofing system to block whining from the little ones and sarcastic comments about the meal from their teenage siblings? Maybe a set of individual cubicles or at least blinders so Child A can't see that Child B got an extra dinosaur-shaped chicken nugget?

Nope. Apparently all we need to "dine with children worry-free" is plastic seat covers to protect the upholstery of our dining-room chairs.

I don't mean to downplay the potential usefulness of such a product, although I would be mystified by any parent who thought that combining small children and upholstered dining-room chairs in the same household was a good idea. All I'm saying is that if our biggest worry about dining with children is whether they might spill on the chairs, we may want to reexamine our priorities.

And so it strikes me about most of the products in the Sky Mall magazine, and indeed many of the things we see for sale in our abundantly blessed era, that they're all about appearances. We seem determined to eliminate or erase or cover up all evidence of the ravages of real life. That's okay, I guess, but I worry about living in a society that takes it to extremes.

For example, I'm in favor of acne medications. I'm all for orthodontia. But when I hear teens bragging about the figure-enhancing surgery they're getting for their sixteenth birthdays, I start to panic. I can envision a world a couple of decades hence in which a regular, unaltered, normally developed body will actually seem freakish.

I'm understanding better every year why President Gordon B. Hinckley encouraged women to take out that second earring (see Hinckley, 97–100). I'll bet it had less to do with the earring itself than with our desire to follow the fashions of the world. It was a way of drawing the line in a safe place, far back from grayer areas that are rapidly spreading in darkness.

So how do we "keep it real" in a world of keeping up appearances? I start by thinking of the friends I love the best. They wear nice clothes—up-to-date, reasonably fashionable, but not extreme and never immodest. They wear makeup and color their hair. But our bodies are all "genuine" (well, except maybe for a few crowns in our teeth). We have laugh lines and age spots and most of us would admit with a twinge that we're packing around a few extra pounds. Few of these friends would likely be called "beautiful" by the world's standards. But if you looked into the eyes of those women for a minute or two, you would see tremendous depth and beauty of soul. They don't just look beautiful, they *are* beautiful. And to be with them is to feel loved and comfortable and happy and understood and enriched.

I've watched enough reality TV to recognize that, given enough money and enough professional help, just about anyone can fake a body. But we can't fake the soul that inhabits it. That's what's real, and it's worth more of our time and attention and devotion than anything we could do to our outsides.

Exercise #17: Keeping It Real

Plan a "shop for your soul" shopping excursion. Instead of buying things to make your body look better, think consciously about what would enhance your spirit. Would it be a book, an inspirational CD, some supplies for a hobby? If your spirit needs a shot of service, then pick up something for someone else. Set up a day when you pamper your spirit the way we're inclined to pamper our bodies, and see how you feel.

CHAPTER
·············

18

Episodes I'm Ashamed Of
An Exercise in Repenting

Do you ever have times when you're really wanting to feel the Spirit, and something flashes into your mind that you did a long time ago that maybe you never really quite repented of, and now it's too late, and you wonder if you're now disqualified forever from feeling the Spirit properly?

Or is it just me?

I remember one such time. It was clear back in high school. I was pretty much a geek in those days, tall and gangly and awkward and shy and precocious with words but clueless in almost every other way. I wasn't part of the top echelon crowd where the cheerleaders and student-body officers and athletes and homecoming royalty lived and moved and socialized. But I had a group of friends among whom wit and wordsmithing were prized enough commodities that I got on all right. We disdained the popular crowd. We mocked them. We were "above" all that jockeying for position and putting on airs and making other people feel inferior. (Hah!) Now I can see that we were just as snobby as we perceived them to be, but about different things. We were all about grades and cleverness and, as I said, using words as both tools and weapons.

One of my friends had a boy in our A.P. English class who was basically infatuated with her. She had kindly tried to let him know that she wasn't interested, but he followed her around faithfully, practically stalking her. We had several intense conversations about what she could do to be rid of him. Finally, I took matters into my own hands. I wrote a very cleverly crafted letter conveying in high-flown terms the message that his attentions were unappreciated and that he should stop bothering my friend. Passing him in the hall one day, I tucked the letter in his shirt pocket and walked on.

When I smugly told my friend later that afternoon what I had done, she was absolutely scandalized. "I can't believe you would do something like that!" she said. "I didn't ask you to do that. I didn't want to hurt his feelings. It wasn't any of your business."

"But . . ." I sputtered. I tried immediately to justify my actions. She obviously was incapable of getting through to him; someone else needed to step in. Maybe he would be hurt for a while, but he'd get over it, and meanwhile she would be rid of him. I had really done both of them a favor. And on and on.

Years later, that scene popped into my mind, and with it a remorse that I could scarcely contain. I couldn't apologize. I couldn't even remember the boy's name. In my attempt to be clever, witty, and smart-alecky, I had hurt an innocent person. And I could never go back and fix that. Ugh. It was a bad, bad feeling.

Come forward in time about thirty years. I was having a really difficult time with a new employee at work. He had been brought in to help in an area of the company in which I had some responsibilities, and because our ways of getting things done were so different, we clashed often. He made me mad, frankly, and I know he upset a lot of others in the company as well, many of whom were my good friends. One day, after yet another blowup, I sat down in frustration and created a silly, oh-so-clever memo that, without naming names, really blasted this guy. I didn't send it all over the company, of course, but I did share it with a few close friends, including my immediate superior. I thought it would make him laugh. I thought he would appreciate the cleverness of it. But what he said was, "Oh, ouch. Don't use your powers for the dark side!"

And *that* brought to mind an incident from a ward choir rehearsal a few years earlier in which I had made some *sotto voce* comment about the bass section that was really more hurtful than clever. In an astonishing act of love and bravery, the choir director, who was my good friend, called me later that afternoon and offered up the kindest rebuke I have ever received: "Someone who is as good with words as you are ought to be able to figure out a way to use them to build people up instead of tearing them down."

Are you seeing a pattern here?

We were talking in Sunday School about how to repent of things that happened so far in our past that we can't really make restitution. One especially spiritually attuned woman suggested, "Repent of whatever quality it was that made you behave that way in the first place." And I realized that I never *had* repented of that quality. I had continued to value cleverness over compassion. I was unforgiving and prone to strike back when I felt threatened, and words were the weapon I wielded.

"Be not deceived," Paul warned the Corinthians. "Evil communications corrupt good manners" (1 Corinthians

15:33). I am working hard to repent of this sin in my life. I'm making a conscious effort to use words to heal rather than to wound, to tease affectionately in ways that allow us to laugh together, to keep my communications honest and aboveboard such that I would never be ashamed to have anything I say heard by my children or my coworkers or my Father in Heaven.

And I am seeing that repenting is a lifelong process that takes attention and sorrow and self-denial and prayer and humility. I'm glad we get to partake of the sacrament every single week to help us keep at it!

Exercise #18: Repenting

The next time some incident pops into your mind that you can't see how to repent of, dig deeper to discover what quality of character was behind the action. Try repenting of that instead. It's harder, but it will serve you better in the long run.

19

Any Spare Change?

An Exercise in Sharing

As in any major city, panhandlers seem to be a permanent part of the landscape in downtown Salt Lake City, where I work. Downtown employees are counseled not to give money to them; it can even be a safety issue if someone sees you pull out your wallet who could easily grab it and run. But it's hard not to feel guilty, especially when someone writes "Mosiah 4:16–18" on the scrap of cardboard he's holding up, and you go home and read that passage of scripture, which is basically about giving your substance to beggars without judging them.

I had a particular challenge with one young woman who had a regular "beat" on North Temple Street, just outside the grounds of Temple Square. Every day, I crossed the street from my parking lot and walked through Temple Square to get to my office, and she approached me nearly every day. I began to dread the encounters, from which I invariably emerged feeling guilty.

I was telling a friend about this and she suggested that, rather than give this woman money, I should find some way to acknowledge her as a person. I determined that I would try this, try to really look at her, smile at her, recognize her as one of God's spirit daughters whom He loved as much as He loved me and my family.

My heart was pounding the next day as I crossed the street. I saw her waiting on the other side, prepared to give me her little speech, which was always the same, "Pardon me, ma'am, do you perhaps have any change you could spare? Anything at all." Instead of hurrying past her, I stopped and looked right into her eyes. I smiled and said, "Good morning. What's your name?"

"Samantha," she said cautiously.

"Hi, Samantha. I've seen you here pretty faithfully every day, haven't I?"

"Unfortunately, yes, that's true."

"Seems to me that someone who could be out here every day in all kinds of weather would probably be a pretty good employee. Have you thought about trying some other kind of work?"

And she launched into a story about the job that was waiting for her as soon as she got some kind of release form from the hospital, and I smiled and thanked her for explaining and wished her good luck, and I went on my way.

When I passed by her "post" on my way home, I smiled at her and said, "Hi, Samantha," and she smiled back a little and waved and that was it. She didn't approach me for money again for a long time. Once, after I had mostly stopped driving to work and so hadn't seen her for a couple of months, she came up to me. I had a granola bar in my pocket, so when she asked for "anything at all," I offered her that. She waved it away, saying, "Oh, I'm diabetic. But thanks anyway."

"No problem," I said cheerfully, and pocketed it again. I never felt guilty after that, and, more important, I never felt a need to avoid Samantha or an uncomfortable feeling that it was selfish of me not to help her. I knew it wasn't "helping" to enable her to live in this fashion. And she knew that she wasn't fooling me, so she stopped even trying.

This new attitude of sharing an acknowledgment of the spirit instead of money opened my heart to try other experiments. I was rushing out from work one day to get to an appointment, and there was a man sitting on the planter box on the corner with the customary "Please help" sign in hand. I had just come from a bake sale in the office and, realizing that I really didn't need the cookies and candy I had bought to support the cause, I walked over and offered the treats to him with a smile. I got a different response this time, as he said, "Sure, that'd be great. Thanks a lot!" I saw him poking through the bag as I drove off, and the thought of the treats he would find gave me pleasure until I remembered that I had taken a huge bite of the Rice Krispies square on my way out of the office and that would be evident to him when he pulled it out of the bag.

Okay, so my giving is not yet perfect. But I am learning that there are lots of ways to give, and that I can be creative about sharing in a way that enriches both me and the recipient. And I'm a lot happier now when I walk down the street!

Exercise #19: Sharing

Assess what you have to give. Choose reputable causes to give money to, and then when someone asks you randomly for a handout you can refuse kindly and without guilt to support his or her ineffective habits. Find a way to acknowledge the person as a sibling in the struggles of mortality, and be sensitive to the nudgings of the Spirit as to what you might share that would be of greater worth than a couple of quarters.

20

How to Schedule an Unsavory Medical Procedure

An Exercise in Practicing Discipline

My dentist called me one day and said, "It's been over two years since you've been in. We have you on our 'inactive list.' Was that intentional?" Two years? How could that have happened? "No, of course not," I said, "schedule me at once." And he did. And he found four cavities, which is kind of what happens if you don't go to the dentist often enough.

I have a new dentist now, with an assistant who greets me cheerfully when I leave the torture chamber—oops, I mean the dental chair—and pulls out her calendar and says, "Six months? Is Wednesday still the best day for you? First thing in the morning?" And she schedules me in and gives me a little card, and I think nothing of it because, after all, six months is an eternity away and my teeth are freshly cleaned now and this time, THIS TIME, I'm really going to be a good flosser.

Well, you know the end to that story. The six months actually fly by, and I haven't flossed like I should, and one day I open my planner to see that I'm going to the dentist on Wednesday (ugh) and of course it isn't convenient and I don't want to go and there are a thousand reasons why it's a bad day for a dentist visit, but it's scheduled and I can't honestly say that it's not possible for me to keep the appointment, so I go. And I'm cavity-free, and my mind is at ease for the next six months.

Here's what I've learned about scheduling something you don't want to do: Just do it. You'll find a way to make it work, and you'll be glad to have it over with.

I have another, more dramatic example of this principle in action. My mother and younger brother both were diagnosed with early stages of colon cancer. Both had successful operations, with not many complications, and needed no further treatment. But if they hadn't had the colonoscopies, the cancer would not have been detected, and it could have been so much worse. In fact, a few months later my dear mother-in-law was diagnosed with the same ailment, but her cancer was advanced and it took her from us two months after the doctors discovered it.

You would think, with this history, that I would be running to the clinic for a colonoscopy, wouldn't you? In fact, with two "primary relatives" having experienced the disease, I am at a significantly higher risk than the general population. Colon cancer is relatively easy to detect and to treat. Polyps can take years to become cancerous, and they can be removed during a colonoscopy, which doesn't even require a surgical procedure. It would be all kinds of foolish of me not to go in and have this test. My parents nagged me. My brother nagged me. And I just couldn't find a time when it was convenient to do it.

Finally, I dug in my heels, called the cancer center, and asked to schedule a colonoscopy. They were busy. This is apparently not a walk-in kind of procedure. But they rummaged around and found me a date two or three months in the future, and I thanked them, and on we went.

Then the month arrived. I turned to May on the calendar and realized that somehow, without noticing it, I had calendared my colonoscopy *one day* before I was scheduled to speak to 5,000 women in the Smith Field House at BYU Women's Conference. This was not good planning. In fact, the temptation to call and cancel the appointment was almost overwhelming. But then I thought, "If not now, when? When is it *ever* going to be convenient for you? When are you ever going to be able to go in without it interfering with some kind of life event? It's not that invasive a procedure; just go in and get it done and then you won't have to think about it again for years."

So I did. And it *was* no big deal (the preparation for the procedure was way worse than the test itself). And I was pronounced clean from any hint of cancer, which is a wonderful thing to be told. And I gave my Women's Conference talk with a light heart because that assignment was checked off my list.

Mammograms are the same kind of assignment for me. They're never going to be fun. They're not likely to ever fall on a day when I didn't have much going on anyway. If I never had to go in for a mammogram the rest of my life, I would be perfectly happy.

But I live in a world where cancer happens. And as unpleasant as mammography can be, it is such a miracle, a blessing that enables doctors to find and eradicate cancer before it totally messes up a person's life. It's worth a little inconvenience and discomfort to partake of that blessing, isn't it?

It's a lesson that goes well beyond medical applications. From organizing the basement to painting the bathroom to dismantling the Christmas tree, my life is filled with things I'm not thrilled about having to do. But I'm always grateful to have *done* them. When such a task rears its head, I know I just need to take a deep breath, put it on the schedule, and keep the commitment. I know I'll be glad I did.

Exercise #20: Practicing Discipline

What is the task sitting in the back of your mind that you *know* you need to get done? Get out your calendar and write it in on a day at least two months in the future. Then, when it comes up on your schedule, resist the temptation to drop it. Just do it! Don't forget to notice how much better you feel after it's done!

21

Automatic Lights

An Exercise in Shining

I came in really early to the office one morning and realized as I stepped off the elevator that I was the first one on
our floor to arrive. That never happens! I'm more of a "come
late, stay late" kind of worker. But I was the early bird that
day, and as I wound my way through the cubicles, there was
kind of an eerie feeling in the building. It was dark—not
pitch-black, of course, but the kind of muted dawn light that
casts everything in gray and makes you want to speak in a
whisper.

Then, as I rounded the corner toward my office, suddenly the whole bank of overhead lights flickered on. It
startled me at first, until I remembered that our office has a

motion-sensing lighting system that turns off the lights when it thinks no one is around and flips them on automatically when someone walks by. The unit can be pretty annoying if you're working late and your cubicle happens to be too far away from the nearest motion sensor in the ceiling. Once, when I had to stay particularly late to finish up a project, I had to get up every eight minutes and walk down the hall a few paces to turn the light back on. I took to tossing out wadded-up pieces of paper as little "motion proxies," but that only worked a couple of times (although it was fun to try).

Anyway, the sudden flood of light in the office that morning set me thinking. What if my own inner light were so sensitive that it could be made to shine by the mere presence of another human being? I have friends—I suspect we all do—who make me smile every time I see them (or sometimes even when I just think of them). How can I attune my "motion sensors" to trigger that kind of light for every human being? Is that even possible?

I think that it is possible, and that maybe we have not just the potential but actually the responsibility to shine. Didn't the Savior command, "Let your light so shine before men, that they may see your good works, and glorify your Father which is in heaven" (Matthew 5:16)? I'm struck by the fact that when we're letting our light shine, it isn't ourselves we're out to glorify. The light we're sharing isn't really ours; it is Christ's.

So how do we get shinier?

The story of Enos offers some helpful insights. Enos apparently hadn't been an especially spiritual man, but one day when he was hunting beasts in the forest he felt that hunger in his soul to feel "the joy of the saints" (Enos 1:3–4). He prayed all day and night until he received the confirmation that his sins were forgiven. Then his thoughts turned to his brethren, the Nephites, and he began to pray for them. After that his love extended even further and he prayed for the Lamanites, who at that time were "wild, and ferocious, and a blood-thirsty people . . . continually seeking to destroy" the Nephites (Enos 1:20). He had learned to shine, not just for the people who "deserved" to feel the light but for everyone he came in contact with.

There seems to be a pattern in the experiences of Enos that might help us in our own efforts to share the light. We have to start by getting ourselves on good spiritual footing. Sometimes it takes a lot of praying to open our hearts enough to feel the love God has always had for us. When we feel it for ourselves, it's natural to want to extend it to our friends, and as we gain experience in sharing that love, it becomes a way of life for us.

The quickest and easiest vehicle for extending inner light is a smile. If the eyes are the windows to the soul, the smile is a window to the heart. It seems to set people immediately at ease, to make them feel welcome, to invite them into your world. It costs nothing, it takes no additional time, but it can open doors in ways you never imagined. Plus, it just feels good.

Letting our light so shine doesn't have to be complicated. It doesn't have to feel like a burden. If you start with a prayer to rev up those spiritual batteries for the day, you'll find that wearing a smile will keep them charged without much difficulty.

Exercise #21: Shining

Pick a day when you're out in public, and make a conscious effort to establish eye contact with and smile at as many strangers as you can. Notice how many of them smile back. You've just shared the light—automatically!

22

Stress Dreams

An Exercise in Worrying

I don't remember my dreams very often, but I have one recurring dream that hits me sometimes when I am under a lot of stress and have something really important brewing that I have to do the next day.

The dream goes something like this: I am on my way to an urgent appointment when my car breaks down. Jumping out, I see that the building I am heading for (it is usually a hotel in my dream, though that is rarely the case in reality) is probably only a mile or so away. If I hurry, I can still get there in time on foot. So I start running down the streets of the city.

The streets get progressively seedier, and I have to keep

stopping, dodging into doorways to avoid unsavory charac-
ters and feeling more and more panicked about arriving
safely. I never do get all the way to the hotel; in fact, it never
gets any closer. I don't ever get accosted, or hurt, or anything;
I just never achieve the goal. And I wake up exhausted.

If dreams are supposed to unravel the cares of the subconscious so that we're able to function in our conscious lives,
what good is a dream like that? All it does is make me more
stressed out than I already was. The only relief is that when
I awake I realize that it was a dream and that I didn't actually
miss my appointment. I guess that's good for something.

It's just sad to me that my mind doesn't deem my conscious worrying sufficient; it invites my subconscious to join
in as well. And it twists reality in such bizarre ways. When my
husband and I were on vacation last fall, I had a dream about
a meeting I was missing at the office. In the dream, I was trying to make a vital point, and my colleague kept interrupt-
ing me with a loud honking noise. At first I tried to laugh it
off. But he persisted. I would just get a good head of steam
under my comments when—"HONK!"—another interrup-
tion. "Come on, now," I pleaded good-naturedly.

"HONK!"

"Just let me finish this one—"

"HONK!"

"This really isn't funny anym—"

"HONK!"

I got so worked up over the nerve of this guy that it woke me up, in which conscious state I soon discovered that my husband was snoring loudly in exactly the same honking tone and intervals as in my dream.

That one made me laugh. But the habit of worrying that precipitates such dreams is anything but funny. Worrying saps our energy, robs our lives of joy, and ultimately makes us dysfunctional.

How can we help it, though? Times are tough. There's so much to worry about. We worry about whether our kids will even have a chance at staying faithful in a world as wicked as ours. We worry about the stability of our employment—even the jobs that seemed the safest are clearly at risk in an uncertain economic climate. We have wars, crime, temptations, and pain of every variety all around us. How can we not be worried?

We can't. But our worries fall in different categories, and being able to recognize those categories can really help us sidestep some of our more irrational and crippling fears.

First, there are things we worry about that we might have some control over. The way to deal with these worries is to spend some quality time thinking about how we might solve them. For instance, I worry a lot about deadlines at work. When I'm the most stressed, I take an hour (and no, I never think I have an hour to spare, but this works every time) and make a detailed list of everything I need to get done. I put the things in order of their priority and set interim goals for myself, and then somehow I'm almost magically able to hack away at the one thing on the top of the list without dragging all the others into it. This works with things like financial planning and time management, worries about allocation of resources that we might have some control over.

Another category of worries is things we have absolutely no control over. I can't fix the conflict in the Middle East. I'm not positioned to heal the economy. I won't be finding the cure for cancer anytime soon. Worries over things in this category have to be turned over to the Lord. If there's anything I can do to help, I trust Him to let me know. I do the little bits of things that I can—helping at the Humanitarian Center, participating in elections, praying for the sick. But I try not to spend too much emotional energy on worrying about this category of things, because no amount of worrying is going to change them; it's just going to make me sick.

A third, and far more nebulous and dangerous category, is worrying about things that *might* happen. I might lose my job. Our dog might get hit by a car. Our daughter might get kidnapped on her way home from school. Our basement might flood, our roof might leak, our dryer might catch on fire, we might have an earthquake . . . the list is endless because the possibilities of what might go wrong in mortality are endless.

I had an experience way back in junior high school that taught me something about dealing with worries of this sort. In order to understand it fully, you have to know what a klutz I was in junior high. Pair an appalling lack of coordination with zero inclination to take physical risks, and you have a twelve-year-old who avoided "tumbling" all the years of her life. Even in sixth grade, when we girls took our slacks to school in paper grocery bags on Friday afternoons in the wintertime so we could do tumbling routines for P.E., I was always the last one in line to execute the forward rolls. Then when the first ones in line came back around for another turn, I let them butt in front of me so I would never get up to the mat. I was just too chicken to be upside down. Ever.

The summer before my eighth-grade year, my parents bought a new house, so we started in a new junior high that fall. It was an awful place where I didn't know the rules and had no friends to teach them to me, and I suffered. The place where I suffered the most (outside of the crowded school bus full of prepubescent village idiots, which is almost too painful to contemplate, even in memory) was in gym class. I was slow. I was clumsy. I was afraid of softballs, volleyballs, and basketballs. I had no flexibility and felt silly trying to do exercise routines. But the worst of all was the six-week unit called "Apparatus." It was just a fancy word for "tumbling," but with the added nightmare of equipment like a balance beam and uneven parallel bars. You can only put yourself at the back of the line so many times in a class like that before the teacher catches on. Mine pulled me aside one day and listened to my tearful confession of my fears. She agreed to give me a "C" if I would show up every day in my gymsuit and at least try to participate. I did, and she made good on her promise.

But, the girls in my class warned me, I would have to figure it out sometime, because in ninth grade everyone had to sign up for a whole *semester* of Apparatus, and the teacher of the class was a gymnastics coach who wasn't inclined to be lenient. I can't tell you the agonies of worry I suffered all through the summertime. It seemed like every time I was prepared to relax and enjoy myself, the thought would buzz back into my head, "Yes, but you know that soon you will be having to take Apparatus."

"Soon" eventually became "now," and I looked my fear in the face as I snapped myself into the standard-issue, one-piece, royal blue gymsuit for my first day of Apparatus. To my relief, we started with a two-week unit on exercise routines. I wasn't great at this, but at least it all took place upright on terra firma.

The inevitable finally arrived, though. We started the tumbling work. I faked headaches in class for a couple of days. I stayed home "sick" for a couple more. And finally my mom, who by now had caught on to what my "sick days" really meant, asked me what was wrong. I told her everything. She took me to talk with the school counselor, who looked at my schedule, heard my story, and said breezily, "Oh, she doesn't *have* to take Apparatus. She just has to enroll in gym." She turned to me and said, "Would you rather do Archery and Square Dancing?" Tears sprang to my eyes at the benevolence of this woman who had, with one swipe of her pen, saved me from disaster. We got the class changed that very day, and I got through the rest of junior high with only minor scarring.

Here, then, is the strategy for worrying about what *might* happen: Get the facts. (And try not to get them from thirteen-year-old girls.) Find out what the possibility really is that such a thing might happen, and educate yourself as to what you could do to soften the blow if it did happen. Earthquake preparedness, food storage, continued education—all of these methods of preparing have been prescribed for years by our

Church leaders as buffers against what *might* happen. Instead of worrying, take action, and even if there's ultimately little you can do, at least you'll spend your time and energy a lot more productively.

Exercise #22: Worrying

Make a list of five things you're afraid might happen. Pick the one that worries you the most, and find out all you can about it. For example, if you're worried about losing your employment, find out what you could do to prepare yourself for an even better job. Make a plan to set aside resources of food and money so that you have a cushion. Study out what you can do to be a more valuable employee, increasing your chances of hanging on through a round of layoffs. Pay your tithing faithfully and ask the Lord to show you how He can open the windows of heaven. Get the idea? Don't worry—act. It's the best remedy there is.

CHAPTER
·············

23

Dandelions

An Exercise in Recognizing
Incremental Progress

I was out in the yard one fine spring day pulling dandelions with my eleven-year-old daughter. We had worked for
more than an hour before I finally stood up to stretch for a
minute. Surveying the yard, I realized that we had barely
made a dent. It made me want to cry. I made some grumpy
comment about how useless this all seemed, and my daughter looked at me for a minute and then said, "Mom, maybe
it's like the hour hand of a clock. You don't really see it move,
but then when you look at it later you can tell that it has."

I know. Way too astute for an eleven-year-old. But still
singularly helpful.

I thought about her comment a lot over the next few

days. We gave up on the dandelions, opting for a good weed-killing fertilizer instead, but I didn't give up on the notion of incremental progress. I began to watch for signs of it in other areas of my life, and was surprised to recognize many times when I hadn't really noticed that I was doing better, but now could see that, in the aggregate, there really was progress.

Don't underestimate the power of the small improvement.

I relearned this lesson one night when my husband and I accepted a ward assignment to help clean the Conference Center. The vastness of that hall when it is empty at 10:00 at night is somewhat overwhelming. We were given the task of vacuuming the seats and floors in one section of the balcony. Larry strapped the vacuum to his back like a Ghostbusters power pack, and I was Cord Woman, following him down the rows with the world's longest extension cord and keeping it wrapped up behind him so it didn't get caught in the seats. We worked a four-hour shift and managed to get ONE section done—one of I don't know how many, but a whole lot of sections. It was like that dandelion-pulling experience—seemingly an exercise in futility.

When the professional supervisor came to relieve us of our equipment and send us home, I asked him, "How on earth do you get it all done?"

He shrugged and answered, "One section at a time."

There's a great lesson in that on how to tackle many of life's jobs. If we had been tasked with cleaning the whole Conference Center that night, we never could have succeeded. It would have taken a huge army of people and a vast quantity of equipment. But with the one-section principle, the work would get accomplished bit by bit, and when they got to the end of the sections they could start back again at the beginning, and on any given occasion the overall effect would have been one of cleanliness.

I've discovered one more area of life in which the concept of incremental progress has served me well, and that is in raising children. Some kids pick things up quickly. They sail along, doing their homework with only a few reminders and deciding on their own at some point to shower and brush their teeth every day and learning to drive and getting jobs and going to dances and all the sorts of things growing children end up doing as the years progress.

And some kids don't. They get stuck for some reason in a certain stage of life and don't seem to move past it. They still have to be encouraged to participate in good grooming habits. They ignore their homework unless nagged almost to the point of murder to work on it. They seem oblivious to the fact that dances are even going on at their school.

Children like the latter can drive their parents to despair. We have visions of them sitting in the living room after their daily four-hour shift at Blockbuster, playing video games and eating Cap'n Crunch out of the box, well into their thirties.

And then one day we notice that for the past while they seem to have been showering and brushing their teeth more regularly. You catch glimpses of the possibility that they have been dating on the sly, though they wouldn't be caught dead admitting it to you. You find their scriptures open on their bed. And you realize that, yes, things are happening. Progress is being made. It's incremental progress, and there are miles to go, but one day that whole yard is going to be free of dandelions, metaphorically speaking.

The hour hand really is moving on.

Exercise #23: Recognizing Incremental Progress

Think of an ineffective behavior that you (or one of your children) used to engage in that you don't anymore. When did you change? Was your transformation sudden or more incremental in nature? How might you make little changes that would add up to big progress in some area of your life?

24

Railroad Crossing

An Exercise in Cultivating Humility

One year, a long time ago, we thought we might like to take a little trip with our kids. We hadn't originally planned to go far, but when we thought about it, suddenly California seemed like a great idea and not that much more trouble and expense. So we unexpectedly found ourselves driving to San Francisco.

We had little children (always a formula for delight on a long drive) and when we realized that we really needed to stop for the night, rather than try to drive straight through, we pulled off the freeway and found a motel and dug in.

The next morning, we were really tired. One hotel room + two adults + three small kids = four hours sleep, max. My husband had done all the driving thus far, so in a burst of generosity I offered to take the wheel. As we were driving out of town, we came to a set of railroad tracks. The railroad crossing warning barriers were closing just as we got to them, and my husband shouted, "Go!"

Well, I just hate it when he tells me what to do when we're driving. And I hate it when he rushes lights and accelerates with excessive force and takes turns faster than I'm comfortable with. So I thought, *You can't tell me what to do,* and I stopped.

"Honey, step on it. Please!" he yelled.

"It says to stop," I replied haughtily.

There was genuine panic in his voice now. "You're on the track! You've got to move!"

Sure enough, I had passed through the first warning gate without seeing it and was now stubbornly stopped right in the path of the oncoming train. I slammed my foot on the gas pedal, gunned it, and we sped past the second gate, feeling it bounce across the roof of the van as we squeaked under it. My heart was racing, the kids were screaming, and the minute we were safe, I pulled over and stopped and made my husband take back the wheel. My hands were shaking as I realized I had truly almost gotten us all killed because I was too prideful and obstinate to listen.

I make excuses for myself when I think about that incident: I was sleep-deprived and didn't see the first gate closing. I misinterpreted my husband's vital warning as an unwelcome attempt to control my driving habits. But the truth was, I was not in the mood to be "dictated to." I was offended that he would accept my offer to drive and then try to tell me how to do it. I wanted to do it *my* way.

I get that way sometimes. I assume that *my* way of doing things is right, or I wouldn't have picked it in the first place, and I get stubborn about accepting input from others whose ways may be just as valid or maybe even better. It's another bad, bad habit that can be filed under the word *pride.* Ever notice how big that file can get?

So I'm working on that. But humility is an elusive quality to try to develop. You can't really encourage yourself by saying, "Look at what a good job I'm doing being humble"; by definition that recognition would be counter to the quality itself.

What *can* we do? Personally, I have to send a red flag up whenever I find myself in a difference of opinion with someone else. My default response is to strategize all the ways I can defend my position and prove that I'm right. I have to make a conscious effort to back off that posture and ask myself, "Why might they be seeing this differently? Are there factors I might not have considered?"

One of the most useful phrases I have learned to use when occasions like this arise is, "Help me understand why you feel the way you do." It is nonconfrontational and non-threatening. It grants others the respect of assuming that they might be correct. It opens the door to further dialogue. It is humble.

It's hard sometimes to hold myself back when I feel strongly about something. But then I remember my van stopped on the railroad tracks, and that motivates me to drop my pride and be saved.

Exercise #24: Cultivating Humility

The next time you feel tempted to line up all your arguments and blast another person with the evidence of how right you are, try instead to ask first, "Help me understand why you feel the way you do." Then, if you end up being right after all, you can preserve the relationship and have your opinion supported openly rather than accepted grudgingly. And if you were wrong . . . well, you just dodged an oncoming train!

25

Wisdom from Gracie

An Exercise in Waiting on the Lord

I'm a collector of sayings. When I find one I particularly like, I post it on the wall of my office to remind myself of the principle. One of my favorites is, "Seize the day! Remember all those women on the *Titanic* who waved off the dessert cart." Another says: "Thousands of candles can be lit from a single candle and the life of the candle will not be shortened. Happiness never decreases by being shared." When I'm extra busy, I alternate between two moods: "My life cannot implement in action the demands of all the people to whom my heart responds," from Anne Morrow Lindbergh, and a line from Jack Nicholson in the movie *As Good As It Gets,* "Go sell crazy somewhere else; we're all full-up here."

I was in a little shop in Maine one year when I picked up a postcard with this saying attributed to comedienne Gracie Allen: "Never put a period where God has placed a comma." It had immediate appeal for me as a person for whom punctuation has been a profession, but its meaning has since gone far beyond the "editing connection."

I like closure. I like to put the period on the sentence of a situation and move on. But life doesn't work that way very often. The Lord frequently invites us to trust Him, to hold on, to endure, to wait and see what He has in mind. As Psalm 27:14 tells us, "Wait on the Lord: be of good courage, and he shall strengthen thine heart: wait, I say, on the Lord."

One of my problems is that, when my patience is tried, sometimes I attempt to jump too quickly to the hindsight. I trust that things will work out all right, and I can wait a little while for events to unfold, but often I try to put the period in places that were obviously meant for a comma. I think I see God's purposes when really we're not there yet.

An example of this was when our oldest daughter was trying to decide whether to serve a mission. It's an easier decision for a young man, I think, because the expectation is there that if he's worthy and able, he'll go. For a young woman, it's a choice, and our daughter felt a keen need to be guided in that decision.

One of her worries was that she might be "supposed" to stay home and get married. She wasn't particularly dating anyone, but she couldn't quite get over that hurdle. Finally I told her, "Sweetheart, why don't you move forward with your papers, and let's see what happens. You know, if you're supposed to get married instead, the Lord can put the man in your path at any moment before you leave, and you can always change your plans at that point."

So she did move forward, and she received her call to the Zimbabwe Harare Mission, and the *next week* the Lord put in her path a young man whom she thought she might be supposed to marry. He was a great guy, more perfect for her than anyone she had ever dated. Everyone in our family loved him. And the agony started all over again. This time she received a clear witness, though, that she was supposed to go, so they said good-bye to each other and she left on her mission.

Her conviction that she had made the right choice was strengthened early on by several choice experiences, including walking into a chapel in Bulawayo where there were people who remembered her great-grandparents when they had served in that exact area more than forty years before. One man even had a painting her great-grandfather had done as a building-fund project that was very similar to one hanging in our living room at home!

She grew so much, and learned so much, and gave so much in return. It was right for her to be there. And when she had been there for about a year, the great young man she had left behind got married. That was hard, but she knew it would be all right because by then she had a firm testimony that serving a mission had been the correct choice for her.

Then she came home, and the flurry of deciding "what's next?" began. It was March, and she wouldn't start school again until September, so she decided to look for a job. She was hoping to get into nursing school the next year, so she took a CNA course and began seeking work in that field. Ridiculously, although there were numerous online postings, she simply could not find a job. She tried and tried. She was reluctant to take a different job because she didn't want to close off the possibility of working in her field of interest, but she just couldn't break into the market.

That was a rough summer. I remember being quite upset with Heavenly Father, and praying, "Isn't she supposed to get blessings for serving Thee? She put everything on the line. Where are her blessings?"

"Wait on the Lord."

One day I was meeting with an author whose book I was editing, and I happened to mention this frustration I had that, in a world where nursing help was supposedly scarce, my daughter couldn't get a job as a certified nurse's assistant. He very graciously offered, "Look, I could use a receptionist in our office. She could still look for a nursing job, and if she only ended up staying three weeks, that would be okay. Why don't you send her out here?" So we did.

She worked there for several months, and they liked her and she liked them, and one day a friend in the office said, "Hey, how would you feel about me setting you up with a friend of mine? He's up at BYU–Idaho, but he's coming down for general conference in a couple of weeks. Will you just meet him?" She agreed, and, to cut to the chase, he was perhaps even more perfect for her than the young man she had left behind, and within a few weeks they were engaged. And she got into a prestigious nursing school on her first try, and now they have two darling children and he teaches seminary and she works as a nurse one shift a week and her blessings are evident to anyone with eyes.

Now the hindsight is clear. She took the path that was right for her. I don't want this to be misinterpreted: I'm not saying every girl should serve a mission. I have heard stories on the other side of the equation, where young women stayed home even after they had received mission calls and received great blessings for doing so. But for *this* young woman, following the Spirit by serving her mission turned the key to her whole life's journey. If she had stayed home, she probably would have gotten married and been happy. But she would not have influenced the lives she did in Africa and in turn had the miraculous mission experiences that will bolster her up all her life. She likely would not have become a nurse. Her life would have been very different.

And, moving forward to that difficult post-mission summer, if she had gotten the blessing we all were praying for and found work as a CNA, she never would have been in a position to meet the choice young man she ended up marrying. He didn't even live in the same city at the time! The hand of the Lord is so evident in the course of events that it just makes my spine tingle.

Here's the kicker: Do I have faith that Heavenly Father loves the rest of my children as much as He loves that daughter? Am I willing to trust Him and wait for *their* blessings to unfold? Or am I so anxious to put that period in place that I get impatient with all His commas?

It's a hard lesson, and I have to learn it over and over, but I'm trusting His promise to strengthen my heart as I wait on the Lord (see Psalm 27:14). I believe the hindsight will come someday!

Exercise #25: Waiting on the Lord

If you're finding that you want the hindsight *now*, try a prayer that asks for strength to be patient instead of for resolution. Ask to be able to endure the commas rather than for the period to be placed. Jot down any insights you're receiving along the path.

26

Am I Sick Yet?

An Exercise in Being Prepared

I am one of those queasy-of-stomach people. On my very first airplane ride, when I was eleven, I threw up. I've almost done it a couple of times since then, once with a very concerned man sitting beside me hollering, "Do you need a mint? Sometimes a mint helps. I've got a mint if you want one. Can I offer you a mint?" I finally took the dang mint just to get him off my back, and it did actually help a little—enough to get us on the ground, anyway.

So when my husband and I were booked to take our first-ever cruise, I was pretty sure I could count on getting seasick. I went to the drugstore weeks in advance and got two kinds of Dramamine (regular and non-drowsy), and then just for good measure I called my doctor and had her prescribe me a little patch some friends had told me about that is worn behind the ear and dispenses a constant dose of anti-nausea medication. (Our cruise director swore that someone asked him once what the religion was of all those people who had the little round stickers behind their ears.)

To my amazement, the motion of the ship didn't affect me in the least. Well, okay, in truth I almost fell over a couple of times when we first set out to sea. The spot on the floor where I had intended to place my foot didn't seem to be there when I set that foot down. But, although I had to learn to tread carefully, I didn't get sick. In fact, it was quite a pleasant sensation to be rocked to sleep at night by the motion of the waves. I ended up not taking any medications at all.

I was chatting about this with some other people in our group and concluded that, although it was kind of frustrating to have spent some money unnecessarily, it had probably been worth it to have the peace of mind. I wasn't afraid of getting seasick because I had plenty of remedies to try if I needed them.

Someone else in the group made a comment that made the principle even clearer: "Instead of begrudging the money you spent for the supplies, maybe you could just rejoice that you didn't need them."

That one really hit home with me. It seemed to open up a whole new avenue of thinking about personal preparedness. So what if my 72-hour-kit has fulfilled no function so far except to gather dust and take up closet space? I'm happy to have it in case I need it, and even happier not to have ever needed it!

Same with #10 cans of pinto beans. And bags of wheat. And water purification tablets. And a whole host of other things that I would be perfectly happy never to need in my life, but that I may be really glad to have someday.

Preparation. It clears away a whole bunch of fears playing in the background of your mind so that you can concentrate on what's going on in the foreground. Whatever it costs, be it money, time, or energy, it's worth it. And if the thing you've prepared so carefully for never ends up happening, so be it. Rejoice!

Exercise #26: Being Prepared

What could you do today to be better prepared in some area of your life? Pick up a few extra cans of tuna or a bag of rice at the grocery store? Try an online recipe that uses whole wheat? Plant something yummy? Don't worry about whether it's "worth" the time or money; just do it, and see if it doesn't give you a little more confidence, a bit more peace of mind.

27

Who, Me?

An Exercise in Finding Your Mission

I have been lucky enough to have a job that I could (and did) keep up with at home part-time for many years. It wasn't always easy to juggle the demands of little children and the deadlines of work, but it was a blessing to be able to add a bit to our income and to keep my oar in, so to speak, in the professional world. When circumstances became such that our family needed me to go back to work full-time, I was prepared to do so almost seamlessly.

Despite my years of part-time experience, I was definitely the junior person on the editing totem pole, so it came as a great surprise when I was called into my boss's office one day and asked to edit what would likely be the most important project we had done or would do for many years. I couldn't imagine why they were asking me. I didn't see how I could do it. I felt frightened and inadequate. And I said yes.

I felt as if I should ask a couple of my colleagues, who understood what that *yes* answer meant, if they would give me a priesthood blessing. Then I began my work. It was difficult, and I needed (and received) a lot of help along the way. But it quickly became evident to me, from the nature of the project and the dynamics of the working relationship with the author, why I had received this assignment. It was clearly not because I was the most experienced editor, or the most skilled. It was because what this project needed more than anything was nurturing. It needed multi-tasking ability. It needed patience. In short, it needed a mom. And I was the only mom on the staff then.

I felt, with that project, a glimmer of insight that the place where I found myself was in fact the spot where I was supposed to be. It was an integral part of my life's mission. That was enormously comforting to me, especially on days when I couldn't do it all—and those days were frequent in the early years—and I sometimes questioned my choices.

As the years have passed and the blessings have flowed, that nugget of insight has grown into a solid conviction. The fact that I am a mother has prepared me in unique ways to serve in the workplace. I remember the staff meetings that I came in for when I was still just working part-time from home. I usually brought my two-year-old with me, and she generally sat on my lap or drew pictures quietly on the bottom couple of inches of the white board. At one such meeting, I was explaining the progress of my current project while my daughter was sitting on my lap flipping my clip-on sunglasses up and down, up and down, on my face. I happened to catch a look at one of the managers in that meeting, and he had the most incredulous expression on his face. It made me laugh when he blurted out, "How can you even be talking with that going on in your face?" I wanted to say, "Honey, if I couldn't work with a little distraction like this, I'd be no good to anybody around *my* house." But I just smiled and said, "I'm used to it."

That ability to work past distractions has served me well. So have my years of experience holding kids accountable for their homework, as now one of my self-titled job descriptions at the office is Deadline Nazi. And in turn, my work has blessed my home life. I can't count the number of times when the very problem I was grappling with at home came up in a manuscript I was working on, and I received the counsel and advice I needed. My life has been enriched and even saved in specific and immediate ways more than once by the authors I have worked with.

This is what I know: If you serve, and you stretch, and you keep trying, the Lord puts your feet on the right path. It's so evident, when we look at the lives of the prophets, that God raises up the right man for the time in which he serves—every single time. Look at President Gordon B. Hinckley's involvement in public relations all through his professional life, and then see the facility with which he interacted with the press throughout his administration. Look at a man who for some years was the only fully functioning member of the First Presidency, and ask yourself if anyone could have done that who hadn't spent a lifetime interacting with the Brethren on various levels.

I think also of President Heber J. Grant, whose business and financial background was so extensive, and how he served as prophet all through the years of the Great Depression. And President Brigham Young, with his organizing genius, was the obvious choice to establish the Saints in the West and direct the migration of thousands to the Salt Lake Valley and surrounding areas.

Look at Joseph Smith's whole life. Why was he, the third son, the one to receive his father's name, when custom would have dictated that the oldest son would have been the candidate for it? (The answer to that question can be found in 2 Nephi 3:6, 15.) Is it possible that the excruciating leg operation he underwent as a boy of seven contributed to his serious and reflective nature as a boy of fourteen? Didn't his family's financial trials drive them right to the spot where he needed to be to experience the religious excitement that led him to the Sacred Grove? And when he went there, the Lord called him by name, demonstrating that He had known Joseph all along.

It's easy to believe that Heavenly Father knows the prophets whom He has prepared to lead us. It may be harder to accept that He knows *our* names too. But it's true. His intimate knowledge of us extends to far before we entered mortality. He knows what we can do, what He needs us to do, and what we'll be the happiest doing. And if we let Him, He'll put us to work serving Him in exactly the ways that make the best use of our abilities. Each of us has a mission to fulfill. The greatest joy in life comes from understanding what it is and doing it.

Exercise #27: Finding Your Mission

Make a list of things you're good at, things you like to do, times in your life when you've felt particularly happy in your successes. Read your patriarchal blessing for further insights. Then ask the Lord what He needs you to do with the interests and gifts you've been given. Act on the promptings you receive!

28

For Best Results

An Exercise in Implementing
the Obvious

I love to read. Always have. I have become, over the years, almost a compulsive reader, taking in everything that has words printed on it. So I've read more than my fair share of product labels, and some of them are pretty funny.

For example, I picked up a bag of candy once that said, "Serving size: ⅕ bag. Servings per container: Approximately 5." Forgive my ignorance if I'm missing something here, but if you divided a bag of *any* size into fifths, wouldn't there automatically be five servings therein?

Another favorite was in the instructions that came with a straightening iron I had bought in a vain attempt to make my hair look the way it did when my hairdresser styled it.

(This never really works, but I never stop trying.) The front of the little instruction booklet said, in bold type, "READ ALL DIRECTIONS BEFORE USING," so of course I had to stop what I was doing immediately and read the booklet before I proceeded to fix my hair. One of the important cautions was: "Do not use while sleeping." To which I say, "Thank goodness I read the booklet before I plugged in the iron! What if I hadn't been aware of that crucial guideline, and had burned my face off or something because I had attempted to use the straightening iron while sleeping?" Honestly! Don't you wonder sometimes what happened that made the manufacturers feel they needed to put a statement like that in their printed instructions?

I had to laugh once when I happened to read the "instructions for use" on a can of that squeezy cheese that you dispense kind of like frosting. We almost never buy that cheese because it's quite expensive and doesn't cover many crackers, but it's nice for long car trips because it doesn't have to be refrigerated, and it's fun to use, so the kids see it almost like a toy—a snack food doubling as an entertainment item. And once we found out that it came out of the car seats pretty well, we stopped worrying and let them have their fun.

Anyway, we had a can left over from a trip and I was sitting at the kitchen counter reading it. The instructions say,

"For best results, remove cap." Sort of a "duh," don't you think? Again, you have to wonder, were they getting calls to that 800 number: "I simply cannot get this cheese to dispense." "Ma'am, did you take the cap off it?" "It has a cap?" Clueless.

Shortly after this we went to church on Sunday, and the opening hymn asked, "Ere you left your room this morning, did you think to pray?" (*Hymns,* no. 140). And I thought, "Duh!" Why do I still, after all these years, seem to need to be reminded? "For best results, start your day with prayer."

Maybe one reason this doesn't always come naturally to me is that "ere I leave my room" in the morning it is generally at a dead run. I have to remind myself that my very busy day is going to go a lot better if I pray about it before I leap into it. I'm trying to be better about this.

That's the real message of the "obvious" instructions in life. There's a reason the Sunday School answers are always the same: read your scriptures and say your prayers. It's because they're the right answers! Duh! I think if we did those two things consistently and effectively every single morning ere we left our rooms, we'd all be a lot calmer.

And maybe, if we're already pretty good at doing those things, we might look at what we could do to step up our commitment a notch. How could my prayers be more

Emily Watts

meaningful? Maybe if I made a sacrifice and got up earlier so I could spend longer thinking and pondering about my prayers, Heavenly Father would honor that sacrifice (as He always seems to) with an increased ability to feel the Spirit. Maybe if I marked my scriptures more carefully or kept a scripture journal or worked harder to memorize a scripture once in a while, the guidance they contain would open up to me a little more clearly. Maybe if I looked past the obvious to the reasons behind it, I could see that it's not a "duh" after all but a "wow!"

Exercise #28: Implementing the Obvious

Think hard about one "obvious" life instruction and decide what you would be willing to do to implement it on a higher level. Don't forget to ponder the blessings that may come as a result of your efforts.

29

Missing My Stop

An Exercise in Living Attentively

As I mentioned in an earlier chapter, I ride the light-rail train to work on most days, and I enjoy reading during the twenty-minute trip. One day on the way home I was so engrossed in a novel that I forgot to pay attention and ended up riding past my stop.

Another time I parked in the morning at a different stop that was about the same distance from my house as my usual stop but was a few blocks closer to town. That afternoon, I got off at my usual stop and began looking for my car before I remembered that it was in a whole different parking lot.

The worst incidence of missing my stop, though, was when I was dozing off but still listening to the automated

voice calling out the stations, and I got off when she/it an-
nounced my stop, only to find that the recording was off and
I had once again gone too far. If I had looked out the window
for even a few seconds, I could have seen this. But I didn't.

Missing my stop is never that big a deal. I just cross over
to the other side of the station and wait for a train going the
other way to pick me up and return me to the missed stop.
But it has been instructive for me in understanding the things
I might be missing when I forget to live attentively.

Sometimes I get so involved in an activity or project or
cause that I lose track of where I am and what I'm supposed
to be doing. In particular, I am too easily distracted from
long-term goals by the allure of the present. This is like missing my stop because I was reading too intently. There's nothing wrong with the activity per se, but it can keep me from
getting where I need to be.

Sometimes I get in a rut. I'm living on autopilot and not
even realizing it. This is like parking in the same place every
day. Again, there's nothing wrong with routines. They free
up our minds from having to keep track of every little
movement, relegating repeated tasks to a barely conscious
level. But if you can't shake off the routine when the occasion
demands it, you're going to miss your stop.

I had a more painful experience with this principle once

when I needed to make twenty-three photocopies of a packet containing forty-two separate sheets. I punched the appropriate buttons on the mega-copy machine in the office and left it churning merrily away. When I returned a few minutes later to collect my packets, imagine my dismay when I discovered I hadn't been paying enough attention, and had neglected to push the proper button to make the machine collate the copies. It was making all the copies of one page individually before going on to the next page, leaving me with 966 sheets of paper that I would have to spend hours collating by hand. I finally decided it would ultimately cost the company less to have me recycle the pages and start over than pay me to walk around a table making twenty-three separate piles of forty-two pages, but it was a real lesson in living attentively.

When you live on autopilot, it drains your creativity and makes you less capable of seeing things in fresh ways. It's less work, but it comes at a cost. Soon life is boring and predictable, and there doesn't seem to be much purpose in it. Life in a rut takes you only one way, and if you don't watch out, you may not realize until too late that it wasn't the way you wanted to go.

In the final example of missing my stop, I abdicated my responsibility to live attentively and relied instead on the instructions of others—instructions that proved to be frustratingly unreliable. It's a lot easier to wait to be told what to do than to have to figure it out on my own, but it seems like a dangerous way to live. What if the person telling you what to do is as clueless as you are?

The only instructions we can truly rely on in our mortal walk are the ones that come from prophets, and even then, we'll be better servants if we pay close attention and understand not just what the instructions are but why they've been given. My default response to prophetic counsel is to assume that it is inspired and then get to work figuring out why it was given. I've always been able to resolve questions to my satisfaction when I've followed this formula.

Living attentively has many benefits. It keeps life exciting. It keeps us on the right path. And it prevents us from making mistakes that might sideswipe us and deter our progress. I'm trying hard not to miss my stop anymore—but at least I know that when I do, I can repent and get back to it!

Exercise #29: Living Attentively

Have a "day of paying attention." Notice the way you do things and ask yourself several times throughout the day, "Is this really the best way, or am I just stuck on autopilot?"

30

How Did This Happen?

An Exercise in Aging Gracefully

I was forty years old before I began to feel my age creeping up on me. Prior to that time, I think I was probably just too busy with little kids to be paying attention. But on my fortieth birthday, I was filled with a need to get away and think about this phenomenon of getting older. Lacking any other outlet, I got in the family van and drove to a vantage point where I could look out over the valley, and I just sat and thought. What was it about this birthday that was so different? Why was I feeling so melancholy?

I finally pinpointed the principal cause of my sadness, and it wasn't quite what I had expected. I realized, as I pondered it, that there were people who had been an important part of my life whom I was never going to see again. Up to that time, I think I had always assumed that the people I really loved would always be a part of my life. We would call. We would get together. We would catch up with each other's lives. On that birthday, I understood that it was not so. I had lost track of friends who had been an integral part of my world, and it made me really sad.

The years kept going on, and one day I realized with a shock that almost all of the new couples who were moving into the apartments in our ward were closer in age to my children than to me. Then colleagues and doctors and all sorts of professionals began to be young enough to be my children, and I started feeling *old*. The worst thought of all was that those people might be looking at me the way I had looked at people in their forties when I was a newlywed. Ugh! How did this happen?

At forty-nine, I became a grandmother, and it is really as wonderful as everyone says it is. For one thing, you get to cuddle and adore and help care for a newborn without being all exhausted from having given birth to it. Christmas and birthdays and trips to the zoo and to the swimming pool become exciting events again. You get the blessing of having little children in your life without the pressure of feeling ultimately responsible for them. Still, the thought of moving up a generation was a bit disconcerting. When I thought of being a grandmother, it was my own grandmother I was picturing, not my mom. And my grandmother was *old*. I was moaning about this to my mother one day, and she said, "Oh, yeah? Try *great*-grandmother."

Now that I'm in my fifties, I'm resigned to the fact that I'm older than many of the people I hang out with. In fact, I kind of like it. It's a calmer age in many ways. I wrote a poem about it once for a friend who had mocked me for getting ancient, a few lines of which I can remember, and I repeat them to myself when I'm feeling particularly decrepit:

> *You youngsters may get all the hype,*
> *But folks prefer a fruit that's ripe.*
> *There are advantages to age:*
> *My kids are past the teething stage.*
> *I don't buy diapers anymore;*
> *I don't drag toddlers to the store.*
> *I'm on good terms with all my chins.*
> *I've given up on "sucking in."*
> *My mortgage payment's pretty small—*
> *I can afford the Geritol. . . .*

And so on. There are lots of things that are fun about being fifty-something. One of them is a little game I like to play called "Remember When?" When I was in my twenties, I never thought I would say this, but now I catch myself saying it all the time.

Remember when girls had to wear dresses to school, and you started a petition to the administration to let you wear slacks?

Remember the first program you ever saw on a color TV? For me, it was a cartoon about Paul Bunyan on *The Wonderful World of Disney*, and I watched it on the set of a neighbor boy across the street.

Remember when Grandma got the first microwave you had ever seen, and she used it exclusively for melting butter?

Remember when you used to ride the bus downtown all by yourself at age nine or ten and wander around the stores and then ride home?

Remember when you wore a one-piece blue gymsuit for P.E., and the girls' gym was completely separate from the boys' gym?

Remember when we went to Sunday School at 10:00 on Sunday morning, came home and had dinner and a good nap, and went back to sacrament meeting at 6:00?

Remember when married couples on TV sitcoms slept in twin beds?

Remember the first time you saw a digital clock?

Remember when no one had cell phones or personal computers? This one is easier for me because I still haven't been able to bring myself to possess a cell phone, but I remember well the first time I did an assignment for work on a computer. I had the thing all typed in but we couldn't get it to print, and I was so *mad!* "If you had just let me use the typewriter," I scolded my husband, "I'd have it in my hand right now to turn in." Yeah, I changed that tune as the years passed.

Remember when we simply couldn't imagine ever needing more than the 64K of RAM in our cutting-edge PC?

I'm used to technology going on without me. "Remember When" is hardly even fun anymore when even my youngest daughter can remember when there was no Internet, no Facebook, no e-mail. But the biggest jolt I've had, oddly enough, came on the day I remembered that back when I was a young bride there was no such thing as ranch dressing.

Young people simply can't believe that's true. Ranch has been the default dressing for so long, the one so universally available in restaurants and at home, that it's hard for them to imagine it hasn't been around forever. But I remember clearly the first time I tasted it, and it wasn't that many years ago.

See? We'll all get old someday. It loses some of its sting when you can remember with fondness all the fun changes in the world. Better start storing things up right now for your own Remember When moments!

Exercise #30: Aging Gracefully

See how many things you can think of that you remember as being new. Are the changes you've experienced universally for the better? Make a list so that you can one day amaze your grandchildren by remembering when . . .

31

Happily Ever After What?

An Exercise in Seizing Happiness Now

My granddaughter is a lover of princesses. Cinderella is her favorite, and long before she could even speak in words that we of this world could understand, she would read her Cinderella storybook to herself, getting all the inflections right and now and then throwing in a word of English, just enough to make it clear that she knew what she was saying even if we couldn't make it out.

One of the phrases that she mastered early was, "And they lived happily ever *after*." This was always pronounced with a lift at the end of the sentence to accompany the satisfying snapping shut of the book. Princesses always live happily ever after, regardless of the dreadful things that happen to them along the way. The question is, what does this mean?

Stephen Sondheim's wonderful musical *Into the Woods* explores in its second half the possibility that "happily ever after" isn't all that the participants in the fairy tales expected it to be. Although they had all achieved the goals that ostensibly were intended to allow them to live happily ever after, what really happened was that they just traded all their old problems for new ones.

I have known for a long time that I can't postpone my happiness. I can't base it on the successful completion of some milestone, because there's always one more hurdle ahead. But, even knowing that, have I really learned to be happy now? I took a survey online recently to help out some BYU students, and one of the questions was, "On a scale of 1 to 10, with 1 being Not Happy at All and 10 being Extremely Happy, how happy are you?"

I thought about it for a while and finally chose 9, because although I do consider myself an Extremely Happy person in general, 10 seemed a little rosy-hued even for me.

But then the next question was, "If you picked any number less than 10, why?"

Hmmm. Why, indeed? What keeps me from being unqualifiedly Extremely Happy? Would I really, truly be *happier* if I weighed less, if I had more energy, if I had more money, if I were more physically fit? I long for those things, but is my happiness actually dependent on them? Is it even important to be at a 10? Wouldn't that remove some of the motivation to keep striving, keep growing, keep aiming to be better?

What really strikes me, though, is that I am finally learning what NOT to base my happiness on. It's not based on how other people behave, since I can't control that. It's not based on what other people think of me, since I can't really control that either. It's not based on having a lack of adversity in my life, because I sure as heck can't control that. President Dieter F. Uchtdorf really hit it on the head in the 2008 general Relief Society meeting when he identified creativity and compassion as the greatest sources of happiness (Uchtdorf, 117–20). Interestingly, both of those are things we CAN control. We get to choose to welcome them into our lives as much as we wish.

Could Christ be "a man of sorrows, and acquainted with grief" (Isaiah 53:3) and still characterize himself as a 10 on the happiness scale? I think He could. I think happiness is one of the attributes God possesses in perfection, but still Enoch saw Him weep. Maybe happiness doesn't imply a total lack of sorrow but a perfect understanding of how to deal with it.

So maybe I *am* a 10 after all; not because my life runs absolutely smoothly but because I choose to find happiness even in the bumps in the road. And maybe being Extremely Happy doesn't imply that there's nothing we would change about our lives—just that we're dealing with what comes our way with creativity and compassion. When we look at it that way, we don't have to wait for any kind of "after." We can be happy right here, right now.

Exercise #31: Seizing Happiness Now

Make two small cards for yourself, one reading "Creativity" and the other "Compassion." Post them in a place where they will remind you to incorporate these elements of happiness into each day. Don't wait for "after"; choose happiness as a way of being *now!*

SOURCES

Hinckley, Gordon B. "Your Greatest Challenge, Mother." *Ensign,*
November 2000.

Hymns of The Church of Jesus Christ of Latter-day Saints. Salt Lake
City: The Church of Jesus Christ of Latter-day Saints, 1985.

Lindbergh, Anne Morrow. *Gift from the Sea.* New York: Random
House, 1955, 1975, p. 118.

Rowling, J. K. *Harry Potter and the Order of the Phoenix.* New York:
Scholastic, 2003.

Uchtdorf, Dieter F. "Happiness, Your Heritage." *Ensign,* November
2008.

ABOUT THE AUTHOR

Emily Watts is a wife, mother of five, and grandmother of three. The author of *Being the Mom: 10 Coping Strategies I Learned by Accident Because I Had Children on Purpose, Take Two Chocolates and Call Me in the Morning,* and *Confessions of an Unbalanced Woman,* she is also a favorite Time Out for Women speaker and an editor for Deseret Book Company.

You can visit her at EmilyWatts.com.